C000264186

the
europhile's
cookbook

EBURY
PRESS

the
wonder
of food

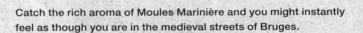

Catch the rich aroma of Moules Marinière and you might instantly feel as though you are in the medieval streets of Bruges.

The crisp and gooey texture of toasted marshmallows might carry you to a campfire beneath the stars in the Lake District. Or the texture of crusty bread and buttery-smooth Brie may whisk you off to a rustic café in a small French market town.

Food transports us. It lets us travel from one time and place to another and from one memory to another in almost no time at all. Thus, Eurotunnel Le Shuttle and food have much in common and it is this wonderful partnership that has inspired us to create this book.

It is, however, a collection of far more than just recipes. It is a combination of discoveries, experiences and stories; contributed by those who have spent the last 25 years travelling and working with us.

In the time it takes you to turn a page, you might travel from one corner of Europe to the next, from one of its mountain ranges to its beaches, from its village cafés and into the countryside. You'll be experiencing everything from a hearty beer and beef stew from the Belgian village of Westvleteren to a traditional, spiced Glühwein that'll evoke memories of German Christmas markets as you go.

So, where will this book transport you?

a flavour of eurotunnel

Ingenious boring contraptions, mid-Channel harbours and horse-drawn stagecoaches.

For almost 200 years, the idea of a cross-Channel tunnel had been talked about, discussed and debated, with all manner of plans and designs being dreamt up. But despite many attempts, and even Napoleon Bonaparte as a supporter, all were abandoned.

But after eight years' work, involving 13,000 engineers and technicians, the centuries old dream was finally realised when, on December 1, 1990, 30m under the English Channel the last piece of rock separating Britain and Europe was drilled away, and an engineering feat few thought possible was achieved. And as the French party journeyed on to Folkestone and the British to Calais, they would become the first humans to walk between the two lands since the last Ice Age.

Amidst flamboyant celebration, ribbon cutting and balloons, the tunnel was officially opened on May 6, 1994 by Queen Elizabeth II and French President Françoise Mitterrand. The two heads of state boarded the Shuttle in the royal Rolls-Royce for the 35-minute

today

The Channel Tunnel was one of the largest construction projects of the 20th Century and even today, at 25 miles, is still the longest under-sea tunnel in the world. Selected as one of the Seven Wonders of the Modern World, it sits alongside some illustrious company including the Empire State Building and the Panama Canal.

Unlike the six other wonders, which soar into the sky or dominate landscapes, the Channel Tunnel is buried 380ft below sea, marble and chalk – meaning many of the wonderful things the tunnel makes possible every day, go unseen. Like the £12bn fruit and veggies travelling through each year, the million express e-Commerce parcels which are carried through every day or the 26 million roses we transport for Valentine's Day alone.

So next time you're getting one of your five-a-day, playing Cupid or opening one of those brown parcels, it might just have made its way to you via this wonder of the modern world.

tomorrow

Since those ribbons were cut and that first royal journey was made, over 80 million vehicles have travelled through the tunnel on Eurotunnel's shuttles.

Whether it's a car, caravan, camper or coach and filled with friends, family, wagging tails or sports equipment, you emerge into Calais just 35 minutes after leaving Folkestone, with all that Europe has to offer within reach. Discovering fantastic cuisine just one of the amazing things to look forward to.

Wine lovers are free to explore the many vineyards and their regimented rows of grapevines at their own pace. Families can surround themselves with the natural beauty off the beaten track and on their own schedule. Sports lovers can follow their team in European football, the Tour de France or head on a pilgrimage in their classic car to Le Mans. While those with an eye for history can lose themselves in the almost innumerable châteaux, churches, gothic architecture and UNESCO World Heritage Sites.

But of course, as a foody and with this recipe book to hand, you can load up your boot with wonderful local produce on the way home, and knock up a dish, dessert or dip that will instantly take you back.

" This is the first time that the heads of state of France and Britain have been able to meet each other without either of them having to travel by sea or by air. "

– Queen Elizabeth II, May 7, 1994.

new ground in sustainability

Before even the first pieces of chalk, marble and shale were dug under the English Channel, a respect for the environment was at the very heart of what Eurotunnel stood for. And has been ever since.

There is no better embodiment of this continued commitment than at Samphire Hoe. This 90-hectare nature reserve, built at the base of The White Cliffs of Dover, is formed entirely from the 5 million cubic tonnes of rock excavated during the construction of the tunnel. Named after the wild Samphire which grows there to this day, the fleshy, green leaves of which were once collected, pickled in barrels of brine and sent to London to be served as a dish to accompany meat.

Today, 21 years after its creation, it is a place where wildlife thrives and is home to over 200 species of plants, including the rare early spider orchid, 120 species of bird, 30 species of butterfly and free roaming cattle.

Looking after the environment means looking to the future too. And Samphire Hoe's new education shelter, built using recycled railway sleepers and spruce cladding, provides a unique and inspiring space for the next generation to learn about, look after and be inspired by nature.

It is testament to our 2,300 employees that Samphire Hoe has been honoured with a Green Flag Award for 13 years running, and that Eurotunnel Le Shuttle remains the most environmentally-friendly way to cross the channel.

"It's the perfect place for a stroll below the White Cliffs of Dover: if you look up you might see kestrels hovering in the sky, look down and there are carpets of wild flowers lining the path."

– Paul Holt, Samphire Hoe Ranger since 1998.

12-13 British Isles

England
Ireland
Scotland
Wales

28-29 France

52-53 Benelux & Scandinavia

Belgium
The Netherlands
Scandinavia

68-69 South-East Europe

Croatia
Greece
Poland
Romania
Serbia
Slovenia

88-89 Spain & Portugal

Portugal
Spain

102-103 Central & Southern Europe

Austria
Hungary
Italy

128-129 Drinks

137 Dog Biscuits

For man's best friend everywhere

140 Index

British Isles

England

14 panettone pudding
with mincemeat & apricots

15 a winter belly warmer
traditional Lincolnshire meat dish

16 steak & ale pies

18 pan-fried hake
with samphire

20 salmon
with grapes, prawns & parsley sauce

22 oysters grilled
with garlic, chilli & cream

Ireland

23 potato farls
griddled potato wedges

Scotland

24 rowies
Aberdeen butteries

Wales

26 bara brith
Welsh "mottled or speckled bread"

panettone pudding
with mincemeat & apricots

Frequent Traveller, Esther Faulkner, says her favourite dessert is Bread and Butter Pudding.
'I like to add my own twist so I spread slices of Italian panettone, rather than ordinary bread,
with mincemeat and add a good slug of brandy to the custard. I use luxury mincemeat as it
has more dried fruit and less liquid.'

Preparation: 15 minutes, plus overnight soaking and standing • Cooking: 30 minutes • Serves 6

ingredients

100g dried apricots, chopped

3 tbsp brandy

a little melted butter, for greasing

10–12 slices of panettone

250g luxury mincemeat

2 eggs

250ml milk

150ml double cream

2 tbsp demerara sugar

method

Put the dried apricots in a bowl and spoon over the brandy. Leave in a cool place to soak overnight. Drain the apricots and set aside, reserving the brandy.

Brush a large ovenproof dish with melted butter. Halve the panettone slices so they fit neatly into the dish, if necessary, and spread them with the mincemeat. Arrange them overlapping in the dish. In a jug, whisk together the eggs, milk, cream and reserved brandy and pour evenly over the panettone slices. Set aside for 15 minutes to give the panettone time to absorb some of the liquid.

Preheat the oven to 170°C (150°C fan)/Gas mark 3.

Sprinkle the demerara sugar over the top and bake the pudding for 30 minutes or until the custard is just set – it should still wobble slightly – and the top is golden and crisp.

Scatter over the chopped apricots and serve warm with homemade vanilla ice cream.

a winter belly warmer
traditional Lincolnshire meat dish

Twice Commonwealth Games Champion, twice the World's Strongest Man and three times an Olympian, no one is going to argue when former shot putter, strong man and Highland Games competitor, Geoff Capes, says he needs plenty of fuel to keep him going. Geoff is also a Frequent Traveller so we didn't need any persuading to include one of his favourite dishes. 'This one comes from the fens of Lincolnshire,' says Geoff, 'an area where the farms are famous for their livestock. Locally it's called 'pig's fry' and it will definitely banish the winter chills.'

Preparation: 15 minutes • Cooking: 4 hours • Serves 4

ingredients

2 medium onions, peeled and chopped

4 pork belly slices

2–3 pig's kidneys

4 slices of lamb's liver

4 rashers of streaky bacon

about 600ml chicken stock

salt and pepper

method

Preheat the oven to 150°C (130°C fan)/Gas mark 2.

Spread out the onions in a baking tray about 7.5cm deep. Lay the pork belly slices on top in a single layer.

Halve the kidneys lengthways and snip out the cores with scissors. Arrange the kidneys, liver slices and bacon rashers over the pork.

Pour enough chicken stock into the tray to just cover all the meat. Season with salt and pepper.

Cover the dish with foil, tucking the foil under the edges of the tray to make a tight seal and cook in the oven for 4 hours.

Serve with new or old potatoes, sprouting broccoli, carrots and peas.

steak & ale pies

One of the stand-out dishes of great British cooking is a steak and ale pie with its golden, flaky crust. Whether you are entertaining friends or simply cooking for the family, it's comfort food like no other. Don't rush cooking the beef, it needs long, slow simmering in its luscious gravy until it is so tender it melts in your mouth. This recipe is for individual pies but make a large one, if you prefer. Just remember there must be plenty of meat hiding under the crisp crust as nobody wants to dig in and find a pie that's half empty!

Preparation: 30 minutes, plus 30 minutes chilling • Cooking: about 3 hours • Serves 4

ingredients

for the filling

3 tbsp oil

600g lean braising steak, cut into 2.5cm cubes

1 large onion, peeled and chopped

3 garlic cloves, peeled and finely chopped

2 tbsp cornflour

500ml rich beef stock

330ml brown ale

2 tbsp tomato purée

1 tbsp fresh thyme leaves

2 bay leaves

salt and pepper

for the crust

500g puff pastry

flour, for rolling out

beaten egg, to glaze

method

Preheat the oven to 170°C (150°C fan)/Gas mark 3. Heat 2 tablespoons of the oil in a large flameproof casserole and brown the steak in batches, transferring the meat to a plate as it browns. Once all the steak is browned, add the remaining oil to the casserole and fry the onion and garlic gently until softened and the onion is turning golden.

Mix the cornflour with a little of the stock until smooth and add to the casserole with the rest of the stock. Stir constantly until the stock comes to the boil and is thickened and smooth. Pour in the ale and when the froth subsides, stir in the tomato purée, thyme and bay leaves. Season with salt and pepper, cover the casserole with foil and a lid and cook in the oven for 2 hours or until the steak is very tender. Set aside and leave until cold.

To assemble the pies, lift the meat from the casserole with a slotted spoon, leaving most of the gravy behind. Divide the meat between 4 individual pie dishes and spoon a couple of tablespoons of gravy into each, reserving the rest for serving.

For the crust, divide the pastry into 4 equal pieces and roll out each piece 5mm thick on a lightly floured surface. Cut strips about 2.5cm wide to fit around the rim of the pie dishes. Brush the strips with water and lift the rest of the pastry on top to cover the filling. Trim the pastry edges with a sharp knife and press them together to seal. Cut a hole in the top of each pie and decorate with leaves cut from the pastry trimmings, fixing these in place by brushing the undersides with water. Lift the pies onto a baking sheet and chill for 30 minutes.

Preheat the oven to 200°C (180°C fan)/Gas mark 6. Brush the tops of the pies with beaten egg and bake in the oven for 25–30 minutes or until the pastry is puffed and golden brown. Serve the pies with the remaining gravy and a selection of vegetables.

pan-fried hake
with samphire

Paul Holt has been the Ranger at Samphire Hoe on the Kent coast since 1998. 'The Hoe was created using 4.9 million cubic metres of chalk marl that was excavated when the Channel Tunnel was dug,' says Paul. 'It's the perfect place for a stroll below the White Cliffs of Dover: if you look up you might see kestrels hovering in the sky, look down and there are carpets of wild flowers lining the path.' In 1994, Eurotunnel and the Dover Express ran a competition to find a name for this land and 'Samphire Hoe', suggested by Gillian Janaway, was chosen. Rock samphire grows on the Hoe and for centuries it's been an important sea vegetable, being mentioned by Shakespeare in King Lear. Today marsh samphire is more popular but both go particularly well with white fish dishes.

Preparation: 15 minutes • Cooking: about 15 minutes • Serves 2

ingredients

2 × 175g hake fillets, skinned

2 tbsp plain flour

2 tbsp olive oil, plus extra for drizzling

30g butter

150g mixed mushrooms, sliced or chopped according to size

100g cherry tomatoes, halved

2 handfuls of marsh samphire

juice of ½ lemon

freshly ground black pepper

method

Dust the hake fillets with the flour.

Heat 1 tablespoon of the olive oil in a frying pan over a medium heat, add half the butter and fry the mushrooms for 3–4 minutes until golden. Add the cherry tomato halves and fry for 1–2 minutes until starting to soften. Remove from the heat and set aside.

While the mushrooms and tomatoes are cooking, bring a pan of unsalted water (the samphire is already salty) to the boil, add the samphire and cook for 1–2 minutes until tender. Drain and add it to the mushrooms and tomatoes.

Heat the remaining olive oil and butter in another frying pan over a fairly high heat and fry the hake fillets for 3 minutes. Carefully turn the fillets over and fry for another 2 minutes.

Reheat the mushrooms, tomatoes and samphire and squeeze the lemon juice over them. Divide between 2 serving plates and top with the hake fillets. Season with freshly ground black pepper, drizzle with a little olive oil and serve.

salmon
with grapes, prawns & parsley sauce

Frequent Travellers, Jim and Jill Byrne, recall eating a dish very similar to this about 15 years ago in a small pub in the heart of Wiltshire. 'At the time, we liked it so much that I decided to try and recreate it myself at home', recalls Jill. 'This is the result and it's still one of our favourite 'special occasion' meals.'

Preparation: 15 minutes • Cooking: 15 minutes • Serves 4

ingredients

50g butter, melted

4 x 175g salmon fillets, skinned

salt and pepper

for the sauce

25g butter

25g plain flour

250ml fish stock

100ml dry white wine

150ml double cream

100g seedless grapes, red or white or a mixture of the two, halved

100g cooked peeled prawns

2 tbsp chopped fresh parsley

lemon wedges, to garnish

method

Line a grill pan with foil and brush it with some of the melted butter. Keep the salmon fillets whole or divide each in half, as preferred. Lay the fillets side by side on the grill pan, skinned side up, brush with the remaining melted butter and season with salt and pepper. Set aside.

To make the sauce, melt the butter in a saucepan. Take the pan off the heat and stir in the flour to make a smooth paste. Cook over a medium heat for 1–2 minutes and then take the pan off the heat and whisk or stir in half the fish stock. When evenly mixed in, add the rest of the stock and the white wine. Bring to the boil, stirring constantly, until the sauce is thickened and smooth. Stir in the cream and leave over a very low heat while you cook the fish.

Grill the fish for 4 minutes, then carefully turn the fillets over and arrange the grapes and prawns around them to heat through. Grill for a further 3–4 minutes or until the salmon flesh is opaque.

Stir the chopped parsley into the sauce and serve the salmon, grapes and prawns with the sauce spooned over.

Garnish with lemon wedges and accompany with mashed or new potatoes and a green vegetable.

England

oysters grilled
with garlic, chilli & cream

Frequent Traveller, Chris Coward, says this is his adaptation of a simple oyster dish.
'It's really cheap and easy – apart from opening the oysters, that is, unless you're an expert!
Basically, it's oysters cooked with cream, chilli, garlic and grated cheese, such as
Parmesan, so, even if you're put off eating oysters raw, I recommend giving these a try
as they are so tasty.'

Preparation: 15 minutes • Cooking: 8–10 minutes • Serves 2 as a starter or light main course

ingredients

12 large oysters

1 large garlic clove, peeled and
grated or finely chopped

1–2 dried chillies, deseeded
and crushed

150ml single cream

3 tbsp grated Parmesan
or a similar cheese such as
Grana Padano

salt and pepper

method

Open the oysters and strain off the liquid in the shells – you may
need to do this twice before adding the rest of the ingredients to
ensure all the liquid has been strained off.

Line a grill tray with foil and arrange the oysters in their shells on
it. Add a little garlic and dried chilli to each, according to personal
taste. Add a spoonful of cream to each shell and sprinkle with
grated cheese. Season with salt and pepper.

Grill for approximately 8–10 minutes or until the oysters are golden
brown and crisp.

Serve at once with a chilled white or rosé wine.

potato farls
griddled potato wedges

'Farl' is a Gaelic word meaning 'four parts' and these griddled potato wedges are an ideal way of using up leftover mashed potatoes. While they are a traditional accompaniment to an Irish fried breakfast, you can also eat them spread with butter or just enjoy them on their own. They are at their best straight from the pan.

Preparation: 20 minutes • Cooking: 6–8 minutes • Makes 4

ingredients

50g butter

450g cold mashed potatoes (about 600g potatoes, if making fresh)

50g plain flour, plus extra for kneading

¼ tsp baking powder

1 medium onion, peeled and very finely chopped

5 spring onions, finely chopped

2 tbsp vegetable oil

salt and pepper

method

Melt 40g of the butter and stir this into the mashed potatoes. Sieve in the flour and baking powder and stir in with the onion and most of the spring onions – reserving a little spring onion for garnish – until evenly combined. Season with salt and pepper.

Transfer the mixture to a floured surface and knead until smooth. Roll or press out into a round, about 23cm (9in) in diameter and cut into quarters with a floured knife.

Heat the remaining butter with the oil in a heavy frying pan or griddle pan and cook the potato farls over a medium heat for 3–4 minutes on each side or until browned. Remove from the pan and serve hot with the reserved spring onion sprinkled over.

rowies
Aberdeen butteries

Preparation: 45 minutes, plus 2 risings for the dough • Cooking: 15–18 minutes • Makes 16

ingredients

500g strong white bread flour, plus extra for dusting

7g sachet of fast-action dried yeast

1 tbsp soft light brown sugar

1 tbsp salt

350ml tepid water

oil, for greasing

275g unsalted butter, diced

100g lard, diced

method

Sieve the flour into a mixing bowl and stir in the yeast, sugar and salt. Make a well in the centre of the dry ingredients and pour in enough of the water in a thin, steady stream, stirring constantly until the mixture comes together, to make a dough – you may not need all the water.

Knead the dough on a lightly floured surface for 8–10 minutes or until it is smooth and elastic. Rub the inside of a large clean bowl with oil, place the dough in it and cover with cling film. Leave in a warm place for at least 1 hour until the dough has doubled in size.

Beat together the butter and lard until combined. Divide the fat into four equal portions and keep in the fridge until needed. When the dough has risen, tip it out of the bowl onto a lightly floured surface and knead again for 1–2 minutes. Roll out the dough to a 40 × 20cm rectangle, about 1cm thick.

With one short side of the dough towards you, spread one portion of the fat over the bottom two-thirds. Fold the top third down and the bottom third up over it, so the dough is now three times its original thickness.

Roll out the dough again to a 40 × 20cm rectangle, 1cm thick, spread with a second portion of fat and repeat the folding process. Do this twice more using the remaining 2 portions of fat, so the dough has been rolled and folded four times.

Roll out the dough again to a rectangle the same size as before and cut it into 16 equal-size pieces. Shape each piece into a flat bun. Line 2 baking sheets with baking parchment and lift 8 buns onto each, well-spaced apart. Cover with a lightly oiled cling film and leave in a warm place to rise until they have doubled in size, about 40–45 minutes.

Preheat the oven to 200°C (180°C fan)/Gas mark 6. Bake the Rowies for 15–18 minutes or until they are golden brown and well risen. Transfer to a wire rack to cool. Serve warm, split and spread with butter and jam.

Eurotunnel's Terminal Planner, Alan Ward, admits this is probably the unhealthiest recipe of all time but that hasn't stopped it being loved by generations of Scots, living in the far north east. 'The origins of the Rowie or Buttery lie with Aberdeen's trawling fleet,' explains Alan, 'and their need for a snack that wouldn't just give them energy and keep out the cold while they were at sea, but was also easy to eat. As bread went stale too quickly, the Rowie roll, made with flour, butter and lard, was created and today it's still a staple in Aberdeen, the rolls being sent to expat Aberdonians around the world who are suffering withdrawal symptoms. This recipe comes from the book: Hairy Bikers' Food Tour Of Britain.'

bara brith

Welsh 'mottled or speckled bread'

Preparation: 30 minutes, plus overnight standing and 4 hours rising
Cooking: 1 hour • Makes 1 loaf

ingredients

225g sultanas

225g raisins

150ml hot black tea

500g strong white bread flour, plus extra for dusting

7g sachet of fast-action dried yeast

1 tsp salt

1 tsp ground mixed spice

75g butter, diced and softened

75g dark soft brown sugar

about 75ml warm milk

1 egg, beaten

oil for greasing

beaten egg or milk, to glaze

method

Put the sultanas and raisins in a bowl and pour over the hot tea. Leave to stand overnight to plump up the dried fruit.

Sieve the flour into a mixing bowl and stir in the yeast, salt and mixed spice. Rub in the butter with your fingertips and then stir in the sugar.

Drain the dried fruit from the tea and pour the tea into a measuring jug. Make up the quantity of liquid to 225ml with warm milk. Mix the milk and tea and beaten egg into the flour mixture and stir to make a soft dough. Turn out onto a floured board and knead the dough until it is no longer sticky. Rub the inside of a clean mixing bowl lightly with oil, place the dough in the bowl and cover with cling film. Leave in a warm place to rise until the dough has doubled in size – about 2 hours.

Knock the dough down with your fist and turn out onto a floured surface. Knead in the sultanas and raisins until they are evenly distributed throughout the dough.

Grease a 900g loaf tin, shape the dough into a loaf and place it in the tin. Cover with a sheet of greased cling film and leave to rise again in a warm place for about 2 hours until the dough rises to the top of the tin.

Preheat the oven to 220°C (200°C fan)/Gas mark 7.

Brush the top of the dough with beaten egg or milk to glaze and bake for 15 minutes. Lower the oven temperature to 180°C (160°C fan)/Gas mark 4 and bake for a further 45 minutes or until golden. If the loaf browns too quickly in the oven, cover the top with a sheet of foil.

When cooked, remove the loaf from the tin – it should sound hollow when tapped on the bottom – and cool on a wire rack. Store in an airtight tin when cold.

Call Centre Team Leaders at Eurotunnel, Sam Rolfe and Laura Wilson, are keen to champion this dark, fruity tea loaf as 'not enough people know just how good it is!' Its Welsh name translates as 'mottled or speckled bread' and Sam and Laura agree there's no better accompaniment to a cup of tea than a thick slice spread generously with butter. Its popularity even stretches as far as Patagonia in Argentina, where it is known as 'black cake'. Not wishing to leave behind their favourite foods, Welsh settlers took the recipe with them when they emigrated to Argentina in the 1860s.

France

France

30   saint nicolas biscuits
traditional Christmas market biscuits

32   porc à la normande
Normandy pork

33   tartiflette
French-style cheesy potato bake

34   scallops baked in the shell
with a mousseline sauce

36   Charlotte aux fraises
strawberry Charlotte

38   tarte porteloise

40   galette des rois
kings' cake

41   dandelion bud 'capers'

42   le roustintin avec le craquelin
kirsch hot chocolate
with crunchy cream puffs

44   cassoulet
slow-cooked sausage & bean stew

46   soupe au pistou
le pistou soup

48   crumbed Reblochon & salad board

49   jollof rice
West African one pot rice dish

50   lamb, chick pea & merguez tajine

saint nicholas biscuits
traditional Christmas market biscuits

'These biscuits are traditionally baked in Calais every December,' says Sabine Veron, Eurotunnel's Civil Engineering Planner. 'They are a speciality of the city and each year we celebrate Saint Nicholas with a Christmas market and a parade. Bakers only sell them from early December until Christmas but I love them so much I bake them all year round. The recipe for the almond biscuit dough doesn't change but I like to experiment with different flavoured frostings, my current being violet.'

Preparation: 30 minutes, plus 1 1/2 hours chilling • Cooking: 8 minutes • Makes 12

ingredients

for the biscuit dough

60g plain flour, plus extra for rolling out

130g icing sugar

150g ground almonds

1 egg

1 tsp liquid glucose or apple sauce

a few drops of almond extract

to decorate

1 egg white

150g icing sugar

decorating icing or piping gel

method

To make the biscuit dough, sieve the flour and icing sugar into a mixing bowl and stir in the ground almonds. Beat the egg and add to the dry ingredients with the liquid glucose or apple sauce and almond extract, bringing the ingredients together to make a soft dough. Knead lightly until smooth and then wrap in cling film and chill in the fridge for 1 hour.

Roll out the dough on a lightly floured surface to 5mm thick and cut out 8cm rounds using a pastry cutter or small, upturned coffee cup. Gather up the dough trimmings to re-roll and cut out more rounds.

Line a baking sheet with baking parchment and lift the rounds onto it. Chill for 30 minutes.

Preheat the oven to 200°C (180°C fan)/Gas mark 6.

Bake the biscuits for about 7 minutes until they still have quite a soft, moist texture. Transfer to a wire rack to cool.

To decorate the biscuits, whisk the egg white until foamy and then gradually whisk in the icing sugar until you have an icing that is still just liquid but thick enough to spread.

Spread the icing over the biscuits with a round-bladed knife. Preheat the oven to 100°C (80°C fan)/Gas mark ¼. Return the biscuits to the baking sheet and put them in the oven for just 1 minute to harden the icing and make it shine.

Pipe the initial 'N' for Saint Nicholas on top of each biscuit with coloured decorating icing or piping gel or the initials of family and friends, if you prefer.

porc à la normande
Normandy pork

Frequent Traveller, Debbie Buck and her husband, Rob, moved to Normandy in 2014 to set up La Crépellière, their luxury *chambre d'hôte* and *gîte* in the beautiful village of Le Menil Garnier. 'Once we were up and running, we decided to offer meals,' says Debbie, 'and, in researching recipes, I came up with my Porc à la Normande recipe. It's easy to do and very forgiving if it's required to stay in the oven for a few extra minutes when serving guests.'

Preparation: 15 minutes • Cooking: 1 hour 20 minutes • Serves 4

ingredients

2 tbsp vegetable oil

4 pork chops

50g bacon lardons

15g butter

3 shallots, peeled and finely chopped

150ml Normandy cider

2 apples, peeled or unpeeled as preferred, cored and cut into slices, or add a chunky apple compote

150ml crème fraîche

salt and pepper

method

Preheat the oven to 190°C (170°C fan)/Gas mark 5.

Heat the oil in a flameproof casserole and brown the pork chops on both sides. Remove from the casserole and set aside.

Add the lardons and fry until lightly browned. Remove and set aside with the pork. Melt the butter in the casserole, add the shallots and fry until softened. Pour in the cider, return the lardons and pork chops to the casserole, cover and cook in the oven for 45 minutes.

Add the apple slices or apple compote, stir in the crème fraîche and season to taste with salt and pepper. Re-cover the casserole and return to the oven for 20 minutes.

Serve accompanied with seasonal vegetables.

France

tartiflette
French-style cheesy potato bake

'This recipe is real cold weather comfort food and it never fails to bring back wonderful memories of the first time I tried it, way back in 1992 when I was on a skiing trip with my class to La Tania, a small resort in France's Les Trois Vallées,' says Frequent Traveller, Sarah Kemp. 'Being able to pop over to France regularly means I can stock up on Reblochon cheese, which gives *tartiflette* its rich, distinctive flavour. It's become a firm favourite in our house.'

Preparation: 15 minutes • Cooking: about 45 minutes • Serves 6

ingredients

1kg waxy potatoes, eg Charlotte, peeled or skins left on, as preferred

200g smoked bacon lardons

1 large onion, peeled and thinly sliced

2 garlic cloves, peeled and finely chopped

100ml dry white wine

450g Reblochon cheese, sliced

200ml double cream or full-fat crème fraîche

salt and pepper

method

Preheat the oven to 200°C (180°C fan)/Gas mark 6.

Boil the potatoes in a pan of boiling, salted water until just tender. Drain and set aside.

Heat a frying pan, add the bacon lardons and dry fry them until their fat runs. When the lardons start to brown, lower the heat, add the onion and garlic and fry until golden brown. Pour in the wine and let it bubble until most of it has evaporated and only a couple of tablespoons remain.

Cut the potatoes into thin slices and layer them in a shallow ovenproof dish with the bacon mixture and half the cheese slices. Pour over the cream, season with salt and plenty of freshly ground black pepper and lay the remaining cheese slices on top.

Bake for 15 minutes or until the cheese is golden and bubbling, finishing with a few minutes under the grill to brown and crisp it.

scallops baked in the shell
with a mousseline sauce

Preparation: 30 minutes • Cooking: 10 minutes • Serves 4 as a starter

ingredients

for the scallops

4 scallops in their shells

8 scallops, white meat only

100g celeriac

juice of ½ lemon

1 carrot, peeled and cut into julienne strips

100g ready-rolled puff pastry

1 egg, beaten

salt and pepper

for the mousseline sauce

3 egg yolks

1 tsp Dijon mustard

1 tbsp white wine vinegar

170g unsalted butter, melted and still warm

2 tbsp chopped fresh tarragon

1 tbsp chopped fresh parsley

100ml whipping cream or double cream, lightly whipped

method

To prepare the scallops in their shells, slide a sharp knife with a thin blade between the two half shells and cut through the large white muscle that attaches the scallop to the shell so the two halves can be prised apart. Using a spoon, scoop out everything inside. Separate the white meat from the outer flesh and discard the rest, including the orange roe.

Rinse all 12 scallops, put them on a plate and cover with paper towel. Chill in the fridge until needed. Wash and scrub the scallop shells thoroughly in hot soapy water, rinse well and dry with paper towel.

Peel the celeriac, cut into julienne strips and toss immediately in the lemon juice to prevent the strips discolouring. Divide the carrot and celeriac julienne between the 4 cup-shaped shells and top each with 3 scallops. Season with salt and pepper and place the flat shells on top.

Preheat the oven to 220°C (200°C fan)/Gas mark 7.

Lay the pastry on a board and cut into 4 strips about 2.5cm wide and long enough to fit around the outside edge of the scallop shells.

Carefully press a pastry strip around each scallop to seal the 2 shells together, gently pushing the strip in position and making sure the seal is tight with no holes. Brush the pastry with beaten egg, place the scallops on a baking sheet and bake for 10 minutes or until the pastry is golden brown.

While the scallops are baking, make the sauce. Put the egg yolks, mustard and vinegar in a blender and process until smooth. With the motor running, gradually add the melted butter until combined to make a smooth sauce. Transfer the sauce to a bowl, mix in the tarragon and parsley and fold in the whipped cream.

When the scallops are ready, place one on each serving plate and either cut through the pastry to open the shells or leave diners to do this. Serve the sauce separately so diners can pour or spoon it over the scallops.

Norma Godfrey is a Eurotunnel Frequent Traveller who says she loves scallops. 'I came across this dish when it was served as a starter at a restaurant near Étaples, Haut de France, and it quickly became a favourite. Unfortunately, the chef retired and it's a few years since I ate it but it lives on in my memory.'

Charlotte aux fraises
strawberry Charlotte

Eurotunnel's Events Coordinator, Julia Champaloux, tells us this very traditional French dessert conjures up lots of memories for anyone who has grown up in France. 'It's the perfect dessert for a hot summer's day and although the cream makes it rich, the strawberries provide the perfect refreshing contrast.'

Preparation: 45 minutes, plus cooling and setting • Cooking: 10 minutes • Serves 6–8

ingredients

for the custard

melted butter, for greasing

450ml milk

4 egg yolks

2 tsp cornflour

50g caster sugar, plus extra for sprinkling

1 tsp vanilla extract

6 sheets of gelatine

3 tbsp orange juice

1 packet of sponge fingers

200ml double cream

2 tbsp orange liqueur

175g strawberries, hulled and sliced

whole or halved strawberries, to decorate

method

Grease a 20cm loose-bottomed round cake tin with melted butter and sprinkle the sides with caster sugar.

To make the custard, heat the milk in a saucepan until it is almost boiling. In a bowl, whisk together the egg yolks, cornflour and sugar until smooth. When the milk is hot, whisk it into the yolk mixture, pour back into the saucepan and stir constantly over a moderate heat until the custard is smooth and slightly thickened. Remove the pan from the heat and stir in the vanilla.

Soak the gelatine sheets in cold water for 5 minutes to soften them. Squeeze the water out of the leaves and place them in a bowl with the orange juice. Stand the bowl over a pan of hot water and leave until the gelatine has melted. Stir into the custard, pour the custard into a bowl and press a sheet of cling film over the surface to prevent a skin forming. Set aside until cold and starting to set.

Arrange sponge fingers around the sides of the tin, sugared side against the tin. Whisk the cream and liqueur together until the cream is just holding its shape and fold into the setting custard. Spoon half the custard into the tin, taking care not to dislodge the sponge fingers, and arrange a layer of sliced strawberries on top. Spoon over the remaining custard and chill in the fridge until firmly set.

Carefully remove the Charlotte from the tin and decorate the top with whole or halved strawberries.

tarte porteloise

'This tart was around long before I was and I hope will be long after I've gone!', laughs José Capez, a Senior Technician at Eurotunnel. 'I've seen my mother make it and she got the recipe from her mother or somebody else. There's no definitive recipe, everyone knows the essentials and adapts the quantities of ingredients accordingly.'

Le Portel is a seaside town about 2 miles southwest of Boulogne and in the fifties and sixties, at the time of a child's first communion, parents prepared these tarts and took them to the local baker's to be cooked in his oven. The tart was then shared with family and neighbours.

Preparation: 45 minutes, plus 1 hour rising for the dough and cooling the custard
Cooking: about 1 hour • Serves 6

ingredients

for the brioche dough crust

250g French T45 flour, type '00' pasta flour or white bread flour, plus extra for rolling out

1 tsp fast-action dried yeast

2 tsp sugar

½ tsp salt

80g unsalted butter, diced

100ml tepid milk

1 egg, beaten

oil for greasing

for the crème libouli filling

600ml milk

1 vanilla pod, split lengthways

3 eggs

150g caster sugar

4 tbsp cornflour

icing sugar, to dust

method

To make the brioche dough, sieve the flour into a bowl, stir in the yeast, sugar and salt and rub in the butter. Add the tepid milk and beaten egg and mix to make a soft dough. Knead for 5 minutes or until smooth, shape into a ball and place the dough in a lightly oiled bowl. Cover with cling film and leave in a warm place to rise for about 1 hour or until doubled in size.

To make the filling, heat the milk and vanilla pod in a saucepan until the milk comes to the boil. Beat the eggs and sugar together, add the cornflour and whisk until smooth. Remove the vanilla pod from the milk and whisk or stir it into the egg mixture. Pour back into the pan and bring to the boil, stirring constantly until the custard is thick and smooth. If lumps start to form, take the pan off the heat and beat hard to break them up. Simmer the custard for 2 minutes, transfer it to a bowl and press cling film over the surface of the custard to prevent a skin forming. Leave until the custard is just warm.

Preheat the oven to 180°C (160°C)/Gas mark 4. Knead the dough again for 5 minutes to burst any air bubbles in it and then roll out as thinly as possible, dusting the work surface and the rolling pin lightly with flour. Line the dough into a 20cm spring-clip tin and spoon in the filling. Bake for 40 minutes or until the crust is golden brown and the filling is set.

When the tart is cooked, dust the top of it with icing sugar and place under a hot grill for a few minutes to brown the custard – protect the pastry with a strip of foil and watch the tart carefully so the custard doesn't burn. Leave to cool completely before removing the tart from the tin.

France

galette des rois
kings' cake

Hannah Tozer is a member of our Customer Relations Team and says she loves this recipe, which was given to her by Eurotunnel's resident French teacher, Christine. 'The galette is made by sandwiching two rounds of puff pastry with frangipane and it is eaten in France on Twelfth Night. Baked inside the galette is a small charm, known as a fève, and whoever finds this charm in their slice, traditionally gets to wear a gold cardboard crown and can name their own king or queen for the day.'

Preparation: 30 minutes, plus 30 minutes chilling • Cooking: about 40 minutes • Serves 6–8

ingredients

75g unsalted butter, diced and softened

60g caster sugar

1 tsp cold water

1 egg, beaten

100g ground almonds

1 tsp rum or brandy

400g puff pastry

2 tbsp apricot jam

beaten egg, to glaze

method

In a mixing bowl, beat the butter until creamy and then beat in the caster sugar until light and fluffy. Mix in the water and beaten egg and stir in the ground almonds and rum or brandy.

Divide the pastry in half and roll each half to a round, 23cm in diameter. Carefully lift one round onto a baking sheet and spread the apricot jam over it, to within 2.5cm of the edge.

Spoon the almond mixture over the jam in an even layer and push your 'fève' into it. Brush the pastry edges lightly with water and lift the second round of pastry on top. Press the pastry edges together to seal and score the pastry top with a sharp knife in a decorative pattern. Brush the pastry with beaten egg and chill in the fridge for 30 minutes.

Preheat the oven to 190°C (170°C fan)/Gas mark 5. Brush the pastry a second time with beaten egg and bake the galette for about 40 minutes until risen, golden and crisp.

France

dandelion bud 'capers'

'We moved to France in August 2016,' says Frequent Traveller, Wendy Clemens, 'and live half an hour from the Eurotunnel terminal in an ancient house with a large wild garden. Last year, there were huge carpets of dandelions growing so I searched around for ways to use the buds and came up with this idea for pickling them like capers. Here is my recipe created from the best bits of ones I tried.'

Preparation: 30 minutes, plus 1 week in the fridge • Makes 1 jar

ingredients

dandelion buds (enough to fill your chosen jar – a jam or honey jar is perfect)

1 tsp finely chopped shallot

1 garlic clove, peeled and finely chopped

2.5cm piece of root ginger, peeled and finely grated

2.5cm piece of turmeric root, peeled and finely grated (if available)

1 bay leaf

4 tbsp clear honey

1 tbsp soy sauce

cider vinegar (enough to fill your jar)

salt and pepper

method

Pick tight dandelion buds well away from roads and dog-walking areas! Give them a quick rinse under cold water and, if you want 'neat' capers and have the time, peel off the leafy bracts. (I've used them with and without the bracts and there's no difference in taste.)

Pack the buds into a sterilised jar, add the shallot, garlic, ginger, turmeric (if you have it, but it's fine without) and bay leaf and season with salt and pepper. Pop the lid on the jar and give the contents a good shake. Add the honey and soy sauce and top up with the vinegar until the jar is full.

Re-seal the jar and store in the fridge for 1 week, shaking it occasionally so the flavours mix together. The 'capers' are ready to eat in a week and are wonderful in salads and cheese sandwiches, with fish, on pizzas or in any other dish where you'd use 'real' capers.

le roustintin avec le craquelin
kirsch hot chocolate
with crunchy cream puffs

Preparation: 1 hour • Cooking: about 45 minutes
Makes about 24 choux buns and enough Le Roustintin to serve at least 4

ingredients

for the craquelin

50g butter, diced and softened

60g demerara sugar

60g plain flour

for the choux buns

75g butter, diced

225ml cold water

125g strong white plain flour

3 eggs

3 tbsp caster sugar

300ml double cream

for le roustintin

500ml milk

75g dark chocolate with 70% cocoa solids, chopped

100ml kirsch

method

To make le craquelin, put the butter in a bowl, add the sugar and beat until combined. Add the flour and mix this in to make a soft dough. Roll out the dough between 2 sheets of baking parchment on a baking sheet until it is 2–3mm thick. Put the baking sheet with the dough still between the parchment sheets into the freezer while you prepare the choux pastry.

To make the choux buns, heat the butter and water in a saucepan until the butter has melted. Bring to a rolling boil and then take the pan off the heat and add all the flour. Beat well with a wooden spoon until there are no lumps and then stir over a low heat until the mixture forms a ball and comes away from the sides of the pan.

Transfer the dough to a cold bowl and set it aside for 5 minutes. Using an electric hand whisk, beat in the eggs one at a time on slow speed until the dough is smooth and glossy, adding 1 teaspoon of the caster sugar with the last egg. Preheat the oven to 200°C (180°C fan)/Gas mark 6.

Line 2 baking sheets with baking parchment, spoon the choux dough into a piping bag fitted with an 8mm plain nozzle and pipe small buns onto the baking sheets. Remove the le craquelin from the freezer and discard the top sheet of parchment. Using a plain pastry cutter the same size as the diameter of the choux buns, cut out the same number of rounds as you have buns. Carefully place one round on top of each bun.

Bake the buns for 25–30 minutes or until golden brown. Remove from the baking sheets and leave on a wire rack to cool. When the buns are cold, whip the cream with the remaining sugar until standing in soft peaks. Split the buns in half through the centre and fill with the cream, either piping it in or using a teaspoon.

When ready to serve, make the le roustintin. Heat the milk in a saucepan until it comes to the boil. Take the pan off the heat and gradually add the chocolate, stirring until the chocolate has melted and is mixed with the milk. Add the kirsch, pour the le roustintin into small cups and serve with the choux buns.

José Capez, a Senior Technician at Eurotunnel, knows just how to keep out the winter chills! 'If you're visiting the Pas-de-Calais when the weather is cold and are tempted by the local hot chocolate – beware – as it will do more than just warm you up! Le Roustintin might look innocent but as well as dark chocolate and milk, it's laced with a more than generous tot of kirsch, which is why it's served in small cups. Such an impressive pick-me-up demands an equally impressive accompaniment and these small choux buns with their crispy topping – known in France as Le Craquelin – are just the thing.'

our tip

If you make the choux buns ahead and they soften before you serve them, pop them back on a baking sheet and re-crisp in a hot oven for 10 minutes

cassoulet
slow-cooked sausage & bean stew

Frequent Travellers, Toni and Kevin Neville, love this hearty dish from south-west France as it reminds them of camp fires and home when they were growing up. 'It's a rough, cheap, one pot meal that can be left to cook for as long as you like,' they say. 'The Toulouse sausages are slowly simmered with bacon, haricot beans, onions, garlic and tomatoes in stock and wine – which must be white – before the crunchy breadcrumb topping is added.'

Preparation: 25 minutes, plus overnight soaking for the beans
Cooking: about 3¼ hours • Serves 4

ingredients

350g dried haricot beans

2 tbsp olive oil

8 Toulouse sausages

100g bacon lardons

2 onions, peeled and chopped

3 garlic cloves, peeled and chopped

1 tbsp fresh thyme leaves

150ml dry white wine

400g can chopped tomatoes

2 tbsp tomato purée

chicken stock

salt and pepper

for the topping

100g fresh white breadcrumbs

3 tbsp chopped fresh parsley

2 garlic cloves, peeled and finely chopped or crushed

method

Soak the haricot beans in a bowl of cold water overnight.

Heat the oil in a large flameproof casserole and fry the sausages over a medium heat until they are evenly browned all over. Remove them from the pan and set aside on a plate. Add the bacon lardons and fry until golden. Remove to the plate with the sausages.

Lower the heat under the casserole, add the onions and cook for about 10 minutes until softened. Add the garlic and thyme, cook for 2 minutes and then pour in the wine. Allow the wine to bubble and reduce a little, return the sausages and bacon to the casserole and add the chopped tomatoes and tomato purée. Pour in enough stock to cover the sausages and beans, season with salt and pepper and cover the casserole tightly with foil and a lid.

Preheat the oven to 150°C (130°C fan)/Gas mark 2 and cook the cassoulet in the oven for 2 hours.

To make the topping, mix together the breadcrumbs, parsley and garlic. Take the lid off the casserole and sprinkle the topping over the cassoulet. Return it, uncovered, to the oven for a further 45 minutes.

soupe au pistou
le pistou soup

Preparation: 20 minutes • Cooking: 30 minutes • Serves 6–8

ingredients

for the soup

2 tbsp olive oil

1 large onion, peeled and finely chopped

2 garlic cloves, peeled and finely chopped

2 medium carrots, peeled and chopped

1 leek, trimmed and sliced

2 medium potatoes, peeled and chopped into small pieces

1 celery stick, chopped

2 courgettes, chopped

600ml vegetable stock

200g French beans, chopped

400g can chopped tomatoes

400g can flageolet beans, drained and rinsed

75g small pasta shapes for soup

coarse sea salt and black pepper

for Le Pistou

4 large garlic cloves, peeled

8 sprigs of fresh basil

4 tbsp grated Parmesan cheese

about 4 tbsp extra virgin olive oil, preferably from Provence

method

Heat the olive oil in a large saucepan over a medium heat, add the onion, garlic, carrots and leek, cover the pan and fry for 5 minutes, stirring regularly.

Add the potatoes, celery and courgettes and fry for 5 minutes. Pour in the stock, add the French beans, chopped tomatoes, flageolet beans and pasta shapes, cover the pan and simmer for 20 minutes or until the vegetables are tender. Taste, season with salt and pepper and add a little more stock or water to the soup if it is too thick.

While the soup is cooking, make Le Pistou. Put the garlic cloves in a pestle and mortar, tear up the basil leaves and add with 1 teaspoon of coarse sea salt. Pound until the garlic and basil are reduced to a purée and then work in the Parmesan and enough olive oil to make a paste.

Serve the soup hot with a spoonful of Le Pistou on top.

'Every year I make three trips by car to Provence,' says Frequent Traveller, Max Davidson. 'I head for the area between Orange and Avignon in the Vaucluse, undulating land that is fringed in the east by the ragged limestone pre-Alps called Les Dentelles and the river Rhône in the west, and where you can find some of the finest and most robust wines in France. I always know I'm back in my 'home from home' when I drop in for lunch at the Hôtel Montmirail in Vacqueyras and Le Pistou is on the menu.'

crumbed Reblochon & salad board

Frequent Travellers, Philip and Yvonne Leaver, regularly use Eurotunnel to visit their daughter who lives on the outskirts of Paris. 'When we're in France there are ample opportunities to eat out,' says Yvonne, 'and at the local wine bar in Marly-le-Roi, where our daughter lives, they serve an excellent charcuterie board. I've tinkered with what they put on it a little, using ingredients that are readily available on this side of the Channel.'

Preparation: 20 minutes, plus 20 chilling
Cooking: 2–3 minutes • Serves 4 – as a starter or light meal

ingredients

for the cheese

1 firm Reblochon cheese

1 egg

10g finely chopped almonds or hazelnuts

2–3 tbsp plain flour

50g fine dried breadcrumbs

oil for deep-frying

to serve

a selection from: thin slices of cooked chorizo, anchovy fillets, rolled slices of jambon cru or pancetta, halved hard-boiled eggs, cherry tomatoes, cornichons – drizzled with vinaigrette (optional)

method

Cut the cheese into 4 equal wedges. Spread out the flour on a plate and beat the egg in a shallow dish. Mix together the breadcrumbs and nuts and spread out on another plate.

Coat the cheese wedges in flour, brush all over with beaten egg and press in the crumb mixture until evenly coated. Chill in the fridge for 20 minutes or longer to firm up the coating.

Heat oil for deep-frying to 180°C and fry the cheese wedges for 2–3 minutes or until golden brown. Drain on a plate lined with kitchen paper and serve with your chosen selection of charcuterie and other accompaniments.

jollof rice
West African one pot rice dish

Frequent Traveller, Anu Gbolasere, grew up in West Africa where this one pot rice dish was his favourite meal as a young boy. 'It brings back memories of my childhood,' says Anu, 'and happily there are plenty of African restaurants in France where it's on the menu.'

Preparation: 30 minutes • Cooking: 1 hour • Serves 4

ingredients

2 large garlic cloves, peeled and roughly chopped

2.5cm piece of root ginger, peeled and roughly chopped or grated

400g can plum tomatoes

1 hot red chilli such as Scotch bonnet, deseeded and roughly chopped

3 tbsp oil

8 chicken thighs, skinned, boned and cut into bite-size pieces

2 onions, peeled and chopped

2 red peppers, deseeded and chopped

500ml chicken stock

3 tbsp tomato purée

240g basmati rice

2 tbsp chopped coriander

salt and pepper

method

Put the garlic, ginger, tomatoes and chilli in a blender and process until smooth. Set aside.

Heat 2 tablespoons of the oil in a large, deep frying pan and sear the chicken pieces in batches over a high heat until they are golden brown all over. Remove the chicken from the pan as the pieces brown and set aside.

Lower the heat under the pan, add the remaining oil and fry the onions and peppers until softened. Pour in the blended tomato mixture and the stock and add the tomato purée. Return the chicken to the pan and simmer uncovered for 15 minutes, stirring occasionally.

Stir in the rice and season with salt and pepper. Cover the pan and cook for 15 minutes or until the rice is tender and has absorbed most of the liquid. Serve with the coriander scattered over.

lamb, chick pea & merguez tajine

'This North African dish is very popular in France,' says Marketing Communications Executive, Rose Joyner. As countries like Algeria were once colonies, a lot of North African people now live in France and there are lots of different recipes for tajines. This one is made with lamb and merguez sausages but chicken is frequently used too.'

Preparation: 30 minutes, plus overnight marinating • Cooking: 3¾ hours • Serves 6

ingredients

600g lamb leg meat, diced

2 tsp paprika

1 tbsp ras al hanout spice mix

1 tsp ground cumin

2 tbsp oil

4 merguez

2 onions, peeled and thinly sliced

2 garlic cloves, peeled and crushed

2.5cm piece of root ginger, peeled and finely chopped or grated

400g can chopped tomatoes

1 tsp harissa paste

400g can chick peas, drained and rinsed

2 carrots, peeled and sliced

300ml lamb stock

1 red pepper, deseeded and chopped

seeds from 1 pomegranate

2 tbsp chopped fresh coriander

salt and pepper

method

Put the lamb in a bowl, add half the paprika, ras al hanout and cumin and toss until the meat is coated with the spices. Cover and chill in the fridge overnight.

Heat the oil in a flameproof casserole and brown the lamb in batches over a high heat. Drain the meat as it browns and set aside on a plate. When all the meat has been sealed, add the merguez and fry until they are browned. Drain and cut each merguez into 2.5cm pieces. Set aside with the lamb.

Add the onions to the casserole, lower the heat and fry until softened. Add the remaining paprika, ras al hanout and cumin, the garlic and ginger and fry for 5 minutes, stirring frequently. Add the chopped tomatoes, harissa paste, chick peas, carrots and stock and bring to the boil.

Preheat the oven to 150°C (130°C fan)/Gas mark 2.

Return the lamb and merguez to the casserole, cover with foil and a lid and cook in the oven for 1 hour. Add the red pepper, season and re-cover the casserole. Cook in the oven for a further 2 hours or until the lamb is very tender.

Serve with the pomegranate seeds and coriander sprinkled over and accompany with cous cous.

For a vegetarian/vegan alternative, replace the lamb and merguez with a selection of vegetables such as courgettes, aubergines, sweet potatoes, pumpkin and green beans. Marinade the vegetables in the spices and brown in batches as per the recipe but reduce the simmering time to about 45 minutes, cooking until the vegetables are just tender.

Benelux & Scandinavia

Belgium

54 waterzooi
creamy fish stew

56 stoofvlees huisbereld met vleteren alt
Belgian beef stew

The Netherlands

58 Dutch apple pie
with a twist

60 zoute haring
salted pickled herrings

62 bitterballen
Dutch meatballs

64 newspaper soup
Dutch carrot soup

Scandinavia

66 gravadlax
with dill & mustard sauce

waterzooi
creamy fish stew

This dish was originally a Flemish fish stew of fresh or salt water fish, carrots, leeks and potatoes simmered in a creamy, white wine sauce but today it can be made with chicken instead. Any type of firm white fish is suitable: we've used hake, but cod, monkfish, sole or halibut would work equally well. Serve with crusty bread to mop up the delicious juices.

Preparation: 15 minutes • Cooking: 35 minutes • Serves 4

ingredients

500g hake fillets, skinned

25g butter

1 onion, peeled and sliced

1 leek, trimmed and cut into matchsticks

1 large carrot, peeled and cut into matchsticks

250g new potatoes, halved or quartered and blanched for 5 minutes

100ml dry white wine

300ml fish stock

100ml double cream

2 tbsp chopped fresh tarragon

salt and pepper

method

Cut the fish into bite-size pieces.

Melt the butter in a pan and fry the onion, leek and carrot for 5 minutes. Add the potatoes, pour in the wine and fish stock and simmer for 20 minutes or until the vegetables are tender.

Add the fish and cook for 5 minutes. Stir in the cream, season with salt and pepper and serve with the chopped tarragon sprinkled over.

stoofvlees huisbereld met vleteren alt

Belgian beef stew

Eurotunnel's Contact Centre Manager, Ian Harrison, says 'about an hour's drive from Calais, just over the Belgian border, is the village of Westvleteren, home to the St Sixtus abbey where the monks brew one of the highest rated beers in the world, Westvleteren XII. It's just one of a number of outstanding beers produced within a 10-mile radius and this traditional Belgian beef stew, served in the restaurant of the hotel Vakantiehoeve Schravenacker in Vleteren, is made with another local beer, Vleteren Alt, brewed at the nearby Deca Brewery.'

Preparation: 30 minutes • Cooking: 2 hours • Serves 6

ingredients

3 tbsp oil

1kg braising steak, cut into 2.5cm cubes

2 large onions, peeled and chopped

3 garlic cloves, peeled and chopped

300ml dark Belgian beer

300ml beef stock

2 tbsp luikse stroop (a Belgian jam made from evaporated fruit juices) or redcurrant jelly

2 sprigs of rosemary

2 sprigs of thyme

3 bay leaves

2 slices of bread

2 tbsp hot mustard

1 tbsp vinegar

salt and pepper

method

Heat 2 tablespoons of the oil in a large flameproof casserole and brown the cubes of steak in batches over a high heat, removing the meat to a plate as the cubes brown. When all the steak has been browned, lower the heat, add the remaining 1 tablespoon of oil and cook the onions gently until they are softened and turning golden.

Add the garlic and cook for 1–2 minutes and then pour in the beer and stock. Stir in the luikse stroop or redcurrant jelly until it has dissolved and add the rosemary, thyme and bay leaves. Season with salt and pepper and bring to the boil.

Spread the bread slices with the mustard and place on top of the stew, mustard side down. Put a lid on the casserole and simmer for 1½ hours. During this time, the bread will disintegrate and will add flavour to the sauce and thicken it.

Remove the lid from the casserole and simmer for a further 30 minutes. Remove and discard the herbs and stir in the vinegar. Serve the stew immediately or – better still – leave it to cool and then refrigerate for 24 hours, with the lid on, so the flavours have time to develop.

Serve with chips and mayonnaise.

Dutch apple pie
with a twist

'This is my Mum's spin on a typical Dutch apple pie,' says Eurotunnel's Planning and Insights Manager, Anne Lous Boeve. 'Don't worry if your pastry is too crumbly to roll out, it's meant to be like that. You just press it out on the baking sheet in an even layer with your hands.'

Preparation: 25 minutes, plus 2–12 hours soaking for sultanas • Cooking: 1 hour • Serves 8–10

ingredients

200g sultanas

250g self-raising flour

250g light muscovado sugar, plus 1 tsp

125g oatmeal

200g butter, plus extra for greasing

750g Bramley apples

1 tsp ground cinnamon

1 tsp lemon juice

3 tbsp muesli

method

Soak the sultanas in cold water for 2 hours, or better still, overnight to plump them up. Drain the sultanas and pat dry with kitchen paper.

In a large bowl, mix together the flour, 250g muscovado sugar and the oatmeal. Melt the butter in a saucepan and stir it into the dry ingredients to make a soft dough, bringing the mixture together with your hand.

Grease a baking sheet by brushing it with melted butter and roll or press out the pastry onto it.

Peel and core the apples and grate them into long strands using the coarse side of a grater. Mix the apple strands with the sultanas, the remaining 1 teaspoon of sugar, the cinnamon and lemon juice, adding a little more spice or lemon juice according to personal taste.

Preheat the oven to 170°C (150°C fan)/Gas mark 3.

Sprinkle the muesli over the pastry and top with the apple mixture, spreading it out evenly. Bake in the oven for about 1 hour or until the pastry is golden brown.

Serve the pie warm or cold with whipped cream and, if wished, scatter a few sweet herb leaves over the top – tiny mint leaves would complement the apples beautifully

Eet smakelijk • Enjoy • Bon appétit!

zoute haring
salted pickled herrings

The Dutch have been eating salted and pickled raw herrings for hundreds of years and they remain just as popular today if the queues at Amsterdam's food stalls in the city's streets are anything to go by. Originally pickling herrings was done for practical reasons as before the arrival of refrigerators and freezers, the fish quickly spoiled. By packing the fillets in barrels of salt, they could be eaten all winter, served with the traditional accompaniment of raw onions.

Preparation: 20 minutes, plus 4 hours curing • Serves 8

ingredients

8 fresh herrings, filleted

coarse sea salt

2 red onions

for the brine

300ml cold water

75ml dry white wine

50ml white wine vinegar

2 tbsp granulated sugar

4 bay leaves

2 tsp coriander seeds

2 tsp fennel seeds

2 tsp juniper berries

method

Lay the herring fillets in a shallow dish in a single layer, skin side down, and cover them with a layer of coarse sea salt. Place a sheet of cling film over the fillets and put a heavy weight – such as a large food can – on top to press down on the fish. Transfer to the fridge and leave the herrings to 'cure' for 4 hours.

Remove the herrings from the dish and rinse each fillet thoroughly under cold running water to remove all the salt. Peel and slice or finely chop the onions.

To make the brine, put the water, wine, vinegar and sugar in a saucepan and heat until the sugar dissolves. Add the bay leaves, coriander seeds, fennel seeds and juniper berries and bring to the boil. Remove from the heat and allow to cool slightly.

Layer up the herring fillets and onions in a large preserving jar until it is full. Pour over the warm brine and seal the jar. When the brine is cold, store the herrings in the fridge and eat within 2–3 days.

bitterballen
Dutch meatballs

In The Netherlands, an evening out with friends will probably start in a café or bar with drinks and tapas-style nibbles, such as these crisp-coated bitterballen meatballs. The 'bitter' part doesn't mean the meatballs have a bitter taste, but instead refers to 'bitters', the alcoholic drinks they accompany.

Preparation: 30 minutes, plus 1 hour chilling • Cooking: 30 minutes • Makes 12

ingredients

2 tbsp olive oil

275g lean minced beef or pork

1 small onion, peeled and finely chopped

¼ tsp freshly grated nutmeg

3 tbsp chopped fresh parsley

finely grated zest and juice of ½ lemon

50g butter

60g plain flour, plus 2 tbsp for coating

225ml milk

1 large or 2 small eggs

75g dried breadcrumbs

oil for deep frying

salt and pepper

method

Heat the oil in a frying pan, add the minced beef or pork and fry until the meat has browned, stirring frequently and breaking up any lumps with the spoon. Remove from the pan and set aside to cool.

Add the onion to the pan and fry until softened but not browned. Remove and set aside as well.

Mix the meat and onion together in a bowl and add the nutmeg, parsley and lemon zest and juice, stirring until everything is combined. Season with salt and pepper.

Melt the butter in a saucepan and stir in the flour off the heat until smooth. Cook for 1 minute and then take the pan off the heat again and gradually mix in the milk. Stir constantly over a moderate heat until you have a thick, smooth sauce. Stir the sauce into the meat mixture and leave to cool.

Using 2 spoons, shape the mixture into 12 even-size balls. Place in a single layer on a plate and chill for 30 minutes.

Spread out the 2 tablespoons of flour for coating on a large plate, beat the eggs in a shallow dish and put the breadcrumbs on another plate. Dust the meatballs in flour, brush with beaten egg and roll in the breadcrumbs until coated all over. Place on a large plate and chill in the fridge for 30 minutes, or until ready to fry, to firm them up.

Heat oil for deep frying to 180°C and fry the meatballs in batches for 3–4 minutes until golden brown. Drain onto a plate lined with kitchen paper and serve at once.

newspaper soup
Dutch carrot soup

Sheila Miller, the mother of our Sales and Marketing Director, Jae Hopkins, sent us the recipe for this soup, which has been a favourite with her family for decades. 'Forty years ago, we swapped our house in Canterbury with that of a Dutch family in Nijmegen,' says Sheila. 'Gerda, the mother, served us this soup, the recipe for which she'd found in a newspaper – hence its unusual name. She emphasised that the soup should be made with 'dirty' carrots, adding that while UK supermarket carrots always seem to be industrially washed, every market in Holland sells carrots with soil still sticking to them. Not only do they keep fresh for longer, they lose fewer of their nutrients and have a better flavour too.'

Preparation: 15 minutes • Cooking: 30 minutes • Serves 6

ingredients

for the soup

2 tbsp olive oil or rapeseed oil

25g butter

500g (dirty) carrots, peeled and sliced

2 large onions, peeled and chopped

3 garlic cloves, peeled and crushed

2.5cm piece of root ginger, peeled and grated or finely chopped

2 tsp curry powder

800ml chicken stock

200ml coconut milk ('a legacy of the influence Indonesia had on Dutch cooking when it was a Dutch colony,' says Sheila)

to garnish

extra coconut milk

fine carrot shavings

method

Heat the oil and butter in a large saucepan, add the carrots, onions, garlic and ginger, cover the pan and cook over a medium heat until the onions are softened but not browned. Add the curry powder and cook for another minute or so.

Pour in the stock and coconut milk and bring to the boil. Lower the heat, cover the pan and simmer for 20 minutes or until the carrots are tender.

Cool a little and then liquidise until smooth. Return to the saucepan and reheat when ready to serve. Top each bowl of soup with a swirl of coconut milk and some fine carrot shavings.

gravadlax
with dill & mustard sauce

'Gravadlax is my go-to recipe for celebrations as it's absolutely delicious, you can make it ahead and it's ideal for feeding a crowd,' says Lisa Emans. 'The salmon must be very, very fresh, preferably sushi grade, so if your fishmonger is unable to supply this, freeze the salmon fillets for at least 24 hours so that any bacteria in the fish are killed. Defrost the salmon when you're ready to prepare the cure. It's worth making double the quantity you think you'll need as there is never enough!'

Preparation: 10 minutes, plus 48 hours curing • Serves 8

ingredients

for the gravadlax

2 × 400g salmon fillets, cut from the thickest part of the fish, skin on

4 tbsp sea salt flakes

60g caster sugar

2 tsp black peppercorns

4 tbsp chopped fresh dill

for the dill and mustard sauce

2 tbsp Dijon mustard

2 tbsp white wine vinegar or cider vinegar

2 tbsp light muscovado sugar

a pinch of salt

2 tbsp vegetable oil

3 tbsp chopped fresh dill

method

To prepare the gravadlax, run your fingers over the salmon flesh to check for any tiny pin bones and pull these out with tweezers. Trim away any thin bits of flesh from the sides of the fillets so they are of even thickness as these will cure too quickly and be unpleasant to eat.

Crush the salt, sugar and peppercorns together in a pestle and mortar or small food processor. Lay 1 salmon fillet in a dish, skin side down, and spread half the chopped dill on top, followed by the sugar mixture. Cover with the rest of the dill and lay the second salmon fillet on top, skin side uppermost.

Place a small board or plate that fits inside the dish on top of the fish and stand a couple of heavy weights, such as food cans, on top. Chill in the fridge for 48 hours, turning the sandwiched salmon over every 12 hours.

To prepare the sauce, whisk together the mustard, vinegar and sugar. Season with a pinch of salt before gradually whisking in the oil. Finally stir in the dill.

To serve the gravadlax, remove the salmon fillets from the dish, separate them and scrape or rinse off the marinade. Slice the flesh diagonally into long, thin slices, leaving the skin behind. Accompany with the sauce and bread – pumpernickel is traditionally served with gravadlax but choose another bread if you prefer.

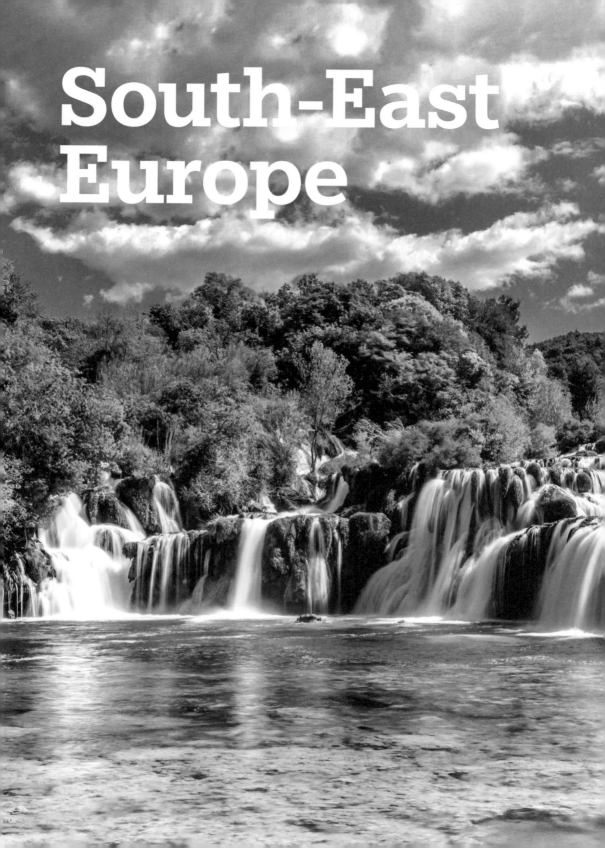

South-East Europe

Croatia

70   plum dumplings

Greece

71   watermelon & feta salad

72   baklava

74   lamb stifado
lamb stewed with onions & red wine

Poland

76   barszcz
beetroot soup

Romania

78   sour cherry cake

80   spring potato salad

Serbia

82   sarma
stuffed cabbage

84   zeljanica
filo pastry pie with spinach

Slovenia

86   Lake Bled cream cake

plum dumplings

This traditional dessert from Croatia is unusual in that the main ingredient in the dumpling dough is mashed potato. The potatoes give them a lovely light texture but it's not a recipe for using up leftover mash, as you need to boil the potatoes in their skins first before peeling and mashing them. Use small, whole plums if they are in season, halving and removing the stones before re-shaping and wrapping them in the dumpling dough. If only larger plums are available, use half to make each dumpling.

Preparation: 15 minutes, plus cooking the potatoes • Cooking: about 25 minutes • Making 10 dumplings

ingredients

450g medium-size floury potatoes, unpeeled

90g plain flour, plus extra for rolling out

2 tbsp semolina

½ tsp ground cinnamon

¼ tsp freshly grated nutmeg

50g butter

1 egg, beaten

10 small plums, pitted and re-shaped, or 5 large plums, halved and pitted

50g dry breadcrumbs

1 tbsp sugar

method

Boil the potatoes in a pan of salted water until tender. Drain and, when cool enough to handle, peel and mash. Stir in the flour, semolina, cinnamon, nutmeg, half the butter (grated or cut into small dice) and the beaten egg to make a dough, adding a little more flour if the mixture is sticky.

Dust a work surface and rolling pin with flour and roll out the dough to about 1cm thick. Cut into 10 equal pieces and mould each piece around a plum to enclose it.

Bring a large pan of water to the boil and add the dumplings. Simmer until the dumplings rise to the surface and then drain with a slotted spoon. Cook the dumplings in batches if you don't have a large enough pan to hold them all.

While the dumplings are cooking, heat the remaining butter in a frying pan and fry the breadcrumbs until they are golden. Transfer to a large plate and sprinkle over the sugar.

Roll the cooked dumplings in the crumbs and serve warm with yoghurt.

watermelon & feta salad

Eurotunnel's Sales and Marketing Director, Jae Hopkins, says 'it's not always easy being a 'veggie' in Europe, although the days when the choice was 'omelette or omelette' are thankfully long gone! Greece is a favourite holiday destination for my family and with all the gorgeous fruit and vegetables they grow, I'm spoilt for choice. This variation on a traditional Greek salad makes the perfect lunch dish, enjoyed on a vine-covered terrace overlooking the deep blue Mediterranean, with a chilled glass of retsina.'

Preparation: 10 minutes • Serves 4

ingredients

½ cucumber, chopped

1 red onion, peeled and thinly sliced

½ small watermelon, peeled and flesh cut into chunks

150g feta cheese, cubed or crumbled

50g pitted black olives

2 tbsp chopped fresh parsley

1 tbsp chopped fresh mint

3 tbsp olive oil

juice of ½ lemon

1 tsp Greek honey

method

Layer the chopped cucumber, red onion slices and watermelon chunks in a serving dish. Scatter over the feta, olives, parsley and mint.

Whisk the oil, lemon juice and honey together and pour over the salad. Toss and serve with bread sticks.

baklava

Preparation: 30 minutes, plus cooling time for the syrup
Cooking: 45–50 minutes • Serves 10–12

ingredients

250g sugar

7 tbsp runny honey

1 cinnamon stick

finely grated zest of 1 orange

100g walnut pieces

100g whole blanched almonds

100g pistachios

2 tsp ground cinnamon

½ tsp ground cloves

190g unsalted butter, melted

12 sheets of filo pastry

method

Put the sugar, honey, cinnamon stick and orange zest in a saucepan, add 300ml cold water and stir over a medium heat until the sugar dissolves. Bring to a simmer and let the syrup bubble for 15 minutes until it has reduced by about one-third. Leave to cool and then remove the cinnamon stick.

Blitz the walnuts, almonds and pistachios together in a food processor until finely chopped. Transfer the nuts to a bowl and stir in the ground cinnamon and cloves. Stir in a couple of tablespoons of the syrup to bind the nut mixture together.

Lightly grease a roasting tin, measuring roughly 33 x 23cm, with melted butter. Cover the filo pastry sheets with cling film and a damp tea towel to prevent them drying out and layer 4 sheets of the pastry into the tin, brushing each one with melted butter.

Spoon over half the nut mixture and layer 4 more sheets of filo on top, again brushing each one with melted butter. Repeat using the remaining nut mixture and last 4 filo sheets, buttering the top sheet generously.

Trim the pastry edges with scissors, if necessary, and, using a sharp knife, cut a diamond pattern through the sheets of filo and filling, going right to the bottom.

Preheat the oven to 180°C (160°C fan)/Gas mark 4 and put a baking sheet on the middle shelf to heat up.

Bake the baklava on the hot sheet for 30–35 minutes or until the pastry is golden brown and crisp. If it looks like browning too quickly, lower the oven temperature to 170°C (150°C fan)/Gas mark 3 for the remaining time.

Remove the baklava from the oven and spoon over half the cold syrup. Leave for 5 minutes for the syrup to settle and run into the cuts in the pastry before spooning over the rest. Leave to cool completely before cutting the baklava into pieces and lifting them from the tin with a palette knife.

Baklava originated centuries ago in the Middle East, its popularity spreading first to Turkey and Armenia and then west to mainland Greece at the time of the Grecian Empire. Made by layering chopped nuts and sweet spices between sheets of filo (also spelt 'phyllo') pastry and pouring over a thick honey syrup when baked, small squares of baklava provide the perfect foil for tiny cups of thick, strong Greek or Turkish coffee. The pastry takes its name from the Greek word for 'leaf', the sheets being as thin as leaves.

our tip Store the baklava in a cool place but not the fridge as the butter brushed over the pastry layers will solidify.

lamb stifado
lamb stewed with onions & red wine

Preparation: 20 minutes • Cooking: 2 hours • Serves 6

ingredients

for the stifado

3 tbsp olive oil

1.5kg lamb, leg or shoulder meat, cut into 2.5cm pieces

250g shallots or baby onions, peeled

4 garlic cloves, peeled and finely chopped

300ml red wine

2 tbsp red wine vinegar

1 tbsp plain flour

200ml lamb stock

400g can chopped tomatoes

2 tbsp tomato purée

1 tbsp clear honey

1 tbsp chopped fresh rosemary leaves

1 tbsp chopped fresh oregano

2 bay leaves

salt and pepper

to serve

3 tbsp chopped fresh parsley

75g feta cheese, crumbled

finely grated zest of 1 lemon

method

To prepare the stifado, heat 2 tablespoons of the olive oil in a large flameproof casserole and brown the lamb in batches over a fairly high heat, removing the pieces to a plate as they brown. Once all the lamb has been sealed, lower the heat and add the shallots or baby onions with the remaining oil. Fry until they are golden all over, add the garlic and cook for a further couple of minutes.

Pour in the red wine and vinegar, mix the flour with a little of the stock until smooth and add to the casserole with the rest of the stock. Bring to the boil, stirring, and then add the tomatoes, tomato purée, honey, rosemary, oregano and bay leaves. Season with salt and pepper.

Preheat the oven to 150°C (130°C)/Gas mark 2.

Cover the casserole tightly with a sheet of foil and the lid and cook in the oven for 1½ hours.

Serve the stifado sprinkled with the parsley, crumbled feta and lemon zest.

Jessica Cole from Eurotunnel's Marketing Department says this hearty lamb stew reminds her of happy holidays spent in Greece. 'Stifado is derived from 'stufado', which was a dish the Venetians brought to Greece in the 13th century,' says Jessica. 'It can be made with lamb or beef but is always slow-cooked and always contains lots of onions and red wine. The lemon, parsley and crumbled feta sprinkled over just before serving provides a tangy contrast to the richness of the gravy.'

barszcz
beetroot soup

It's called Barszcz in Poland, Barŝĉici in Lithuania and Borscht in the Ukraine but by whatever name you know it, there's no doubting that this is one of eastern Europe's most popular soups. 'The landlord's stepmother was Polish. She would always be busy in the kitchen rustling up incredible dishes for her family and friends to enjoy. One of my favourites was this very tasty beetroot soup,' says Lisa Emans – Senior Business Analyst at Eurotunnel.

Preparation: 15 minutes • Cooking: 45 minutes • Serves 4–6

ingredients

1 tbsp vegetable oil

15g butter

1 medium red onion, peeled and finely chopped

1 celery stick, cut into small dice

1 large carrot, peeled and cut into small dice

3 garlic cloves, peeled and finely chopped

350g raw beetroot, peeled and cut into small dice or grated (see our tip)

1 large potato, peeled and cut into small dice

1.5 litres well flavoured beef stock

½ small red or green cabbage, finely shredded

salt and pepper

to serve

sour cream

chopped fresh dill

method

Heat the oil and butter in a large saucepan and fry the onion, celery, carrot and garlic over a low heat until softened but not browned.

Add the beetroot and potato and fry for 2–3 minutes, stirring regularly. Pour in the stock, bring to the boil and then lower the heat and simmer for 15 minutes. Add the shredded cabbage, season with salt and pepper, cover the pan and simmer for 15 minutes or until all the vegetables are tender.

Serve the soup topped with sour cream and sprinkled with chopped fresh dill.

 our tip Peeling and chopping or grating beetroot is a messy business so, if you prefer not to end up with purple hands for days, wear thin disposal gloves.

 dietary tip Although traditionally made with strongly flavoured beef stock, the soup can be made with vegetable stock if preferred.

sour cherry cake

'Every family in Romania has a recipe for this cake as it's so popular,' says Eurotunnel Administrative Assistant, Miruna Tomescu. 'It has a firmer texture than a traditional English sponge and reminds me so much of home when summer arrived and I used to spend Sundays with my family. Mum and I would bake this cake and I now continue this tradition with my son. It's not an elaborate cake, it's easy to make and you can use any fruit that is in season, such as strawberries, plums, blackberries or apricots.'

Preparation: 25 minutes • Cooking: 45 minutes • Serves 8

ingredients

oil for greasing

300g plain flour, plus extra for dusting

2 tsp baking powder

175g caster sugar

finely grated zest of 1 lemon

50ml sunflower or rapeseed oil

60g butter, melted and cooled

4 eggs

1 tsp vanilla extract

200g natural Greek yoghurt

300g sour cherries, pitted (well drained and patted dry with kitchen paper if using canned cherries)

method

Preheat the oven to 180°C (160°C fan)/Gas mark 4. Brush the base and sides of a 20cm round cake tin with oil and line with baking parchment.

Sieve the flour into a mixing bowl with the baking powder and stir in the sugar and lemon zest. Beat together the oil, melted butter, eggs, vanilla and yoghurt and stir into the dry ingredients until everything is evenly combined.

Pour the mixture into the tin, spreading the top level. Dust the cherries lightly with a little extra flour and spoon them over the top of the cake. Dusting them with flour helps prevent them sinking down into the batter.

Bake the cake for about 45 minutes or until risen and golden brown on top. Cool in the tin for 15 minutes before turning it out onto a wire rack to cool completely.

spring potato salad

Miruna Tomescu is an Adminstrative Assistant at Eurotunnel and she recommends this colourful alternative to an English potato salad. 'I call it a 'spring' potato salad but, as long as you start with potatoes, you can vary the other ingredients according to what's in season,' she says. 'At home, we always made it with potatoes, olives, onions, eggs and – if it was spring – added radishes and spring onions but that was just us giving the salad a modern twist.'

Preparation: 30 minutes • Cooking: 15–20 minutes • Serves 4

ingredients

for the salad

200g new potatoes, washed but unpeeled

4 eggs

1 red onion, peeled and thinly sliced

12 small pickled gherkins, sliced

4 spring onions, trimmed and chopped

75g pitted black or green olives (or a mixture of the two), sliced or left whole

6 radishes, sliced

1 roasted red pepper from a jar, thinly sliced

2 tbsp chopped fresh chives

2 tbsp chopped fresh parsley

for the dressing

3 tbsp extra virgin olive oil

1 tsp mustard, eg Dijon

1 tbsp white wine vinegar

salt and pepper

method

To prepare the salad, cook the potatoes in a pan of boiling, salted water until they are just tender, about 15–20 minutes depending on their size. Drain and set aside to cool before slicing or just cutting in half if the potatoes are very small.

Meanwhile, put the eggs in a small saucepan, cover them with cold water and bring the water to a fast boil. Immediately lower the heat under the pan and simmer the eggs for 7 minutes. Drain straight away, run cold water over the eggs to cool them and place in a bowl of cold water. When the eggs are cold, drain, peel off the shells and slice or cut the eggs into wedges.

Put the potatoes, sliced onion, gherkins, spring onions, olives, radishes, red pepper slices and half the chives and parsley in a large bowl.

To make the dressing, whisk 1 tablespoon of the olive oil into the mustard until smooth and the two are evenly combined. Repeat with another tablespoon of oil and, when combined, do the same with the remaining tablespoon. The mixture should now have the consistency of mayonnaise. Dilute by stirring or whisking in the vinegar and then add the remaining chives and parsley. Season with salt and pepper.

Serve the potato salad straight from the bowl or spoon it onto a serving platter, pour over the dressing and toss everything together until coated in the dressing. Top with the hard-boiled eggs.

dietary tip

For a vegan alternative, replace the hard-boiled eggs with cherry tomatoes, grated courgettes, carrot julienne or baby corn.

sarma
stuffed cabbage

A traditional Serbian dish where cabbage leaves are stuffed with minced meat, rice and spicy paprika and then layered in a casserole before being slowly braised in a tomato and vegetable stock. In Serbia, pickled cabbage leaves would be used but they can be replaced with fresh leaves, if pickled ones are difficult to find. Layering fresh cabbage parcels with sauerkraut provides the distinctive sour flavour.

Preparation: 20 minutes • Cooking: 50 minutes • Serves 6

ingredients

12 outer leaves from 1 large cabbage, eg savoy

250g lean minced beef

250g lean minced pork

150g long grain rice

1 onion, peeled and finely chopped

4 tsp paprika, plus extra for sprinkling

1 egg, beaten

450g sauerkraut, drained and rinsed

vegetable stock mixed with 2 tbsp tomato purée

salt and freshly ground black pepper

method

Blanch the cabbage leaves in a large pan of boiling water for 2 minutes until they are limp. Drain and cool under cold water. Pat the leaves dry with kitchen paper and set aside.

In a large bowl, mix together the minced beef, pork, rice and onion. Stir in the paprika, season with salt and freshly ground black pepper and stir in the beaten egg – this prevents the cabbage leaves unwrapping during cooking.

Divide the meat mixture between the cabbage leaves, spooning a little into the centre of each. Fold the sides of the leaves over the filling and roll up to make tight packages. Spoon half the sauerkraut into a flameproof casserole and layer the cabbage leaves on top. Cover with the rest of the sauerkraut, sprinkle over a little paprika and top up with vegetable stock so the parcels are covered.

Heat until the stock is just coming to the boil, lower the heat, cover the pan tightly and simmer gently for 45 minutes so the liquid is only just bubbling.

Vegetarians can replace the minced beef and pork with vegetables, dried fruits and nuts. Mix a selection of raw vegetables such as grated carrots, tiny cauliflower or broccoli florets, finely diced courgettes, chopped red peppers and mushrooms with chopped dried apricots, dried cranberries or raisins and a few flaked almonds or chopped pistachios.

zeljanica
filo pastry pie with spinach

A vegetarian dish that's popular all over the Balkan States and Greece, where it is known as Spanakopita. The crisp filo crust encloses a tangy filling of spinach, ricotta, soured cream and feta cheese and the pie can be served warm or cold as an appetiser, light lunch or supper dish accompanied with a mixed salad. Although major supermarkets sell filo pastry, if you have a Greek, Turkish or south-east European food store near you, it's worth buying your filo there as you'll get a lighter, flakier result.

Preparation: 30 minutes, plus 15 minutes cooling • Cooking: about 1 hour • Serves 6

ingredients

300g young spinach leaves

175g ricotta

175ml full fat soured cream

225g feta cheese, crumbled

½ tsp freshly grated nutmeg

5 eggs, beaten

100g butter, melted

4 large sheets of filo pastry

2 tbsp sesame seeds

salt and pepper

method

Rinse the spinach and place in a large pan with just the rinsing water clinging to the leaves. Cover the pan and cook over a medium heat for 3–4 minutes or until the spinach wilts. Drain, pat the leaves dry with kitchen paper and coarsely chop them.

Put the spinach in a large bowl and add the ricotta, soured cream, feta and nutmeg and stir until mixed. Add the beaten eggs, then season with salt and pepper, again mixing well.

Brush a 20cm spring-clip tin with melted butter and layer the sheets of filo pastry into the tin, brushing each one with melted butter and letting excess pastry hang over the sides of the tin. Spread the spinach mixture evenly into the tin and fold the overlapping sheets of filo over the filling to enclose it. Brush the filo with the remaining butter, sprinkle over the sesame seeds and lift the pie onto a baking sheet.

Preheat the oven to 180°C (160°C fan)/Gas mark 4.

Bake the pie for 50–60 minutes or until the pastry is golden brown and the filling is set. Leave to cool for 15 minutes before removing carefully from the tin. Serve warm or cold.

Lake Bled cream cake

Preparation: 1 hour, plus 2½ hours chilling for the pastry and custard
Cooking: about 40 minutes • Serves 8

ingredients

for the pastry layers

500g puff pastry

flour, for rolling out

beaten egg, to glaze

for the custard

1 litre milk

2 tbsp plain flour

6 eggs, separated

70g caster sugar

1 tsp vanilla extract

for the cream topping

450ml whipping cream or double cream

2 tbsp caster sugar

1 tsp vanilla extract

icing sugar, to dust

method

To make the pastry layers, divide the pastry in half and roll each half to a square about 5mm thick. Lift the squares onto baking sheets, prick them all over with a fork and chill for 30 minutes.

Preheat the oven to 200°C (180°C fan)/Gas mark 6. Brush the pastry squares with beaten egg to glaze and bake them for about 15 minutes or until crisp and golden brown. Remove from the oven and place another baking sheet on top of each square to flatten it. Neaten the pastry edges with a sharp knife, trimming each piece to a 20cm square. Set aside to cool.

To prepare the custard, heat 750ml of the milk in a saucepan until bubbles appear on the surface. Meanwhile, whisk the flour with the rest of the milk in a large jug until smooth. In a mixing bowl, whisk the egg yolks, sugar and vanilla together until thick and creamy. In a separate bowl, whisk the egg whites until standing in firm peaks.

When the milk in the saucepan is hot, whisk it into the cold milk and flour and then gradually whisk in the egg yolk mixture. Pour back into the saucepan and cook over a medium heat, stirring constantly until the custard is smooth and starting to thicken. Take the pan off the heat and fold in the egg whites, 1 tablespoon at a time. Return to the heat and cook the custard over a low heat for 10 minutes or until it has thickened, stirring from time to time.

Put 1 pastry square upside down in the base of a 20cm square cake tin and pour over the warm custard. Leave to cool and then chill for about 2 hours to give the custard time to set.

To make the cream topping, whisk the cream with the sugar and vanilla until thick. Spread the cream evenly over the custard in the tin and top with the other square of pastry right side up.

Chill until ready to serve. Carefully remove the cake from the tin, dust the top with icing sugar and serve cut into portions with a sharp knife.

Eurotunnel's Senior Business Analyst, Ljiljana Rosier, says her favourite holiday destination is Lake Bled in Slovenia. 'The Park Café is home to the original Lake Bled cream cake and, while there are now many variations of this popular pastry, the one served at the café is still the best. Sitting on the terrace eating a slice of the cake and taking in the breath-taking view across the lake is an unforgettable experience,' she says.

Spain & Portugal

Portugal

90   pastéis de nata
Portuguese custard tarts

92   arroz de marisco
shellfish with rice

Spain

94-95   tapas

     aioli

     patatas bravas

     albondigas
     Spanish meatballs

98   pimientos de padrón

100   Spanish chicken
with chorizo, peppers & olives

pastéis de nata
Portuguese custard tarts

These totally irresistible little tartlets with their flaky crust and rich custard filling were first made in the 18th century by the monks of the Jerónimos Monastery in the parish of Santa Maria de Belém, Lisbon. In those days, it was common for egg whites to be used to starch clothes with the leftover yolks being turned into creamy custards and other desserts. After the monastery closed in 1834, the recipe was sold to a sugar refinery in Belém and the descendants of the company's original owners are still in charge of it today.

**Preparation: 45 minutes, plus 30 minutes chilling and 15 minutes freezing
Cooking: 30 minutes • Makes 12**

ingredients

melted butter, for greasing

375g sheet of ready-rolled puff pastry

100ml whole milk

1 tbsp cornflour

150ml double cream

75g caster sugar

finely grated zest of 1 small lemon

2.5cm piece of cinnamon stick

4 egg yolks

½ tsp vanilla extract

method

Brush a 12–cup tartlet tray generously with melted butter and chill in the fridge for 30 minutes.

Unroll the pastry, remove the parchment and carefully roll the pastry back up again. Using a small sharp knife, cut across the roll to make 12 equal spirals. Press each spiral flat into a cup in the tray, starting it at the centre, so it spreads up the sides and fills the cup. Prick the pastry cases with a fork and put the tray in the freezer for 15 minutes.

Preheat the oven to 220°C (200°C fan)/Gas mark 7. Remove the pastry cases from the freezer and bake them for 5 minutes or until pale golden. Press each case down in the centre where the pastry has puffed up to flatten it. Increase the oven temperature to 230°C (210°C fan)/Gas mark 8.

Whisk the milk and cornflour together until smooth. Heat the cream in a small saucepan with the sugar, lemon zest and cinnamon stick until the sugar has dissolved. Bring almost to the boil, remove from the heat and lift out the cinnamon stick – it can be rinsed and dried and used for another recipe.

Whisk the egg yolks, whisk in the milk and cornflour and then pour on the hot cream, whisking all the time. Pour the mixture back into the saucepan and stir constantly over a medium heat until the custard has thickened – don't let it boil as this will make it too thick. If any lumps start to form, take the pan off the heat and whisk the custard briskly to break them up. Pour the custard into a jug and stir in the vanilla.

Carefully fill the pastry cases with the custard and return the tarts to the oven for 15 minutes or until the custard is puffed and scorched in places. Cool the tarts for 10–15 minutes in the tray before removing to a wire rack to cool and giving the filling time to sink back down.

arroz de marisco
shellfish with rice

Platform Coordinator, Carlos Silva Marques, is rightfully proud of his country's cuisine and especially this dish, which, he says, 'is easy to prepare, full of flavour and a 'must-try' for anyone visiting Portugal'. Considered to be among the country's 'top 7 gastronomic wonders', it makes the most of local seafood and can include prawns, lobster, clams, cockles, crab, mussels and squid.

Preparation: 30 minutes • Cooking: 40 minutes • Serves 4

ingredients

2 tbsp olive oil

1 onion, peeled and sliced

3 garlic cloves, peeled and finely chopped

2 tsp paprika

4 tomatoes, peeled and chopped

125ml dry white Portuguese wine

225g long grain rice

500ml fish stock

225g mussels in their shells, cleaned

225g clams in their shells, cleaned

225g squid, cleaned and cut into rings

8 large, raw prawns, peeled

juice of ½ lemon

1 tbsp chopped fresh oregano

salt and pepper

method

Heat the oil in a large sauté pan with a lid and fry the onion and garlic over a medium heat until they are soft and golden brown. Add the paprika, fry for 1 minute and then add the tomatoes and pour in the wine. Simmer for 5 minutes so the wine reduces a little.

Stir in the rice, pour in the stock, cover the pan and simmer for about 10 minutes or until the rice is nearly cooked.

Add the mussels, clams, squid and prawns, cover and cook for about 15 minutes or until the shells of the mussels and clams have opened and the squid and prawns are opaque.

Season with the lemon juice, salt and pepper, stir in the oregano and serve at once.

tapas

Jackie Goldfinch is Eurotunnel's Customer Relations Administrator and when she was younger, she lived in Spain. 'I have very fond memories of going to our local tapas restaurant with my Dad,' recalls Jackie. 'We would order a selection of dishes, plus aioli and some crusty bread, and spend the afternoon chatting and sharing food. My Dad has sadly passed away but I still eat tapas as they remind me of Spain and the happy times I spent there with him. These, and the Albondigas recipe overleaf, are a few of my favourites. Each will each serve 4 people as part of a selection of tapas.'

tortilla Española

ingredients

6 large eggs

oil for frying

5 medium potatoes, peeled and cut into 3mm slices

2–3 medium onions, peeled and chopped

salt and pepper

method

Beat the eggs vigorously in a bowl with a large pinch of salt until frothy. Heat about 2.5cm oil in a large frying pan over a medium heat. Add the potatoes and onions, lower the heat and cook them for about 25 minutes – the oil should only gently bubble – until the vegetables are tender. Lift the potatoes and onions from the pan with a slotted spoon and drain on a plate lined with kitchen paper. When they are well-drained, transfer them to a bowl and season generously with salt and pepper, stirring well to combine.

Beat the eggs again and then scrape in the potatoes and onions. Set aside for 5 minutes. Drain all but 3 tablespoons of oil from the frying pan. Place over a medium-high heat and add the egg mixture. Cook, swirling the pan rapidly until the bottom and sides of the tortilla are set, about 3 minutes. Lower the heat and cook for a further 3 minutes.

Carefully upturn the tortilla onto a large plate, add another tablespoon of oil to the pan and slide the tortilla back in. Cook for about 2 minutes, pressing the sides in with a spatula to neaten them.

Cook until a skewer pushed into the centre of the tortilla comes out clean and then slide the tortilla out of the pan onto a serving plate. Leave to stand for at least 5 minutes before cutting into wedges or cubes. Serve warm or at room temperature.

aioli

ingredients

6 tbsp mayonnaise

2 large garlic cloves, peeled and crushed or grated

salt

method

Mix the mayonnaise with the garlic, stir in 2 teaspoons of cold water and season with a pinch of salt. Serve with crusty bread, prawns or raw vegetables for dipping.

patatas bravas

ingredients

400g potatoes, unpeeled and cut into bite-size pieces

oil for drizzling and frying

1 tbsp tomato purée

½ tsp chilli flakes

1 tomato, diced

chopped fresh parsley, to garnish

salt, pepper and a pinch of sugar

method

Preheat the oven to 200°C (180°C fan)/Gas mark 6. Spread out the potatoes in a shallow roasting tin, drizzle with oil and season with salt and pepper. Roast in the oven for 25–30 minutes or until golden and crisp. Dissolve the tomato purée in 100ml hot water and add the chilli flakes. Heat 1 tablespoon of oil in a large frying pan over a medium heat, add the diced tomato and season with salt and a pinch of sugar. Cook for 3–4 minutes until the tomato has broken down. Add the tomato and chilli stock and cook for a further 3–4 minutes. Transfer the cooked potatoes to a serving dish and spoon over the tomato sauce. Garnish with chopped parsley.

albondigas
Spanish meatballs

Preparation: 30 minutes, plus 1 hour chilling • Cooking: 30 minutes
Serves 4 – as part of a selection of tapas dishes – or 2 as a main course

ingredients

for the meatballs

250g minced beef

250g minced pork

4 garlic cloves, peeled and finely chopped

1 small onion, peeled and finely chopped

1 tbsp chopped fresh parsley

1 slice of bread, torn into small pieces and soaked in milk

1 egg, beaten

olive oil for frying

salt and pepper

for the tomato sauce

1 tbsp olive oil

½ onion, peeled and finely chopped

2 garlic cloves, peeled and chopped

4 large tomatoes, diced

5 tbsp tomato purée

1 tsp smoked paprika

¼ tsp dried thyme

1 tbsp clear honey

2 tbsp chopped fresh oregano

method

To make the meatballs, mix all the ingredients (except the oil) together in a bowl until evenly combined and season with salt and pepper. Cover the bowl with cling film and chill the mixture in the fridge for 30 minutes. Dampen your hands and roll the meat mixture into 20 walnut-size balls, place on a plate in a single layer and chill for a further 30 minutes or until ready to cook. Shallow fry the meatballs in a little olive oil, turning them regularly so they are browned on all sides. Drain onto a plate lined with kitchen paper.

To make the tomato sauce, heat the oil in a saucepan large enough to take all the meatballs and fry the onion and garlic over a low heat until softened. Add the tomatoes, simmer until they are soft and then stir in the tomato purée, smoked paprika, thyme and honey. Season with salt and pepper and taste to see if the sauce needs more honey or pepper. Add the meatballs to the pan and simmer gently for 10 minutes. Serve sprinkled with the oregano as part of a tapas spread. If serving as a main course, accompany with crusty bread, pasta or rice.

'Serve these Spanish-style meatballs in spicy tomato sauce with my tapas on the previous page and you'll have a simple but delicious spread for family or friends,' says Jackie Goldfinch, Eurotunnel's Customer Relations Administrator. 'You could also serve them as a main course for two people.'

dietary tip

Vegetarians can replace the meat with lentils, kidney beans or chick peas, plus extra vegetables such as grated carrots, sweetcorn kernels and chopped spinach. If using chick peas, blitz them briefly in a food processor to reduce them to a coarse meal. Spices, ground or finely chopped nuts and grated lemon zest could also be added for extra texture and flavour. If serving as a main course, try courgette 'spaghetti' as an accompaniment.

pimientos de padrón

These small green chilli peppers from Spain are a particular favourite of Eurotunnel Driver/ Chef de Train, Alan Hughes. 'The peppers are briefly fried in hot oil until crisp then sprinkled with coarse salt and served as a starter or part of a tapas spread,' says Alan. 'They were originally a speciality of Galicia but now you'll find them all over Spain – I discovered them in Lanzarotte. Unlike normal chillies, the peppers are mild, although the odd hot one does creep in and you don't know which one it is until you've bitten into it!'

Preparation: 5 minutes • Cooking: about 2 minutes • Serves 4

ingredients

250g pimientos de padrón

3 tbsp light olive oil or vegetable oil

coarse sea salt

method

Leave the peppers whole with their stalks on. Rinse and pat them dry with a clean tea towel or kitchen paper.

Heat the oil in a heavy frying pan large enough to take all the peppers in a single layer.

When the oil is very hot, add the peppers and fry, without stirring, for about 45 seconds or until their skins are blistered underneath. Turn the peppers over and fry for a further 1 minute or until they are blistered all over – they should be soft on the inside but their skins crisp.

Sprinkle the peppers with coarse sea salt and transfer them to a serving dish. Sprinkle with a little more salt and serve at once, on their own or as part of a tapas spread.

Spanish chicken
with chorizo, peppers & olives

Margaret Finch, Eurotunnel's API Agent, has discovered some wonderful chicken dishes on her trips to Spain. 'This recipe is a particular favourite,' says Margaret, 'as it's extremely tasty, very colourful and all the ingredients are cooked in one pot – exactly my kind of dish as it saves on the washing up! As a variation, you could tuck fresh orange wedges among the chicken and vegetables 20 minutes before the end of cooking time.'

Preparation: 20 minutes • Cooking: 1 hour • Serves 4

ingredients

8 chicken thighs on the bone, skin on

2 tsp smoked paprika

3 tbsp olive oil

100g chorizo, cut into rounds

225g small new potatoes

2 red onions

1 red pepper

1 yellow or orange pepper

1 green pepper

4 large garlic cloves, left whole with skins on

juice of 1 lemon

3 tbsp chopped fresh oregano

1 tbsp chopped fresh thyme

freshly ground black pepper

100g pitted black olives

4 tomatoes, cut into quarters

75ml dry sherry

method

Dust the chicken thighs with the paprika and lay them in a single layer in a large roasting tin. Drizzle with 1 tablespoon of the olive oil and add the chorizo to the tin. Halve the potatoes, peel and cut the onions into wedges and deseed and chop the peppers.

Put all the vegetables in a large bowl and add the remaining olive oil, stirring them around so they are coated. Tip the vegetables into the roasting tin around the chicken and tuck the garlic cloves among them.

Squeeze over the lemon juice, add 2 tablespoons of the oregano and all the thyme and season with plenty of black pepper. Preheat the oven to 180°C (160°C fan)/Gas mark 4 and roast for 45 minutes. Turn the vegetables over, add the olives and tomato quarters to the tin and spoon the sherry over the chicken. Roast for a further 15 minutes or until the chicken is cooked and the vegetables are tender. Serve with the remaining oregano sprinkled over.

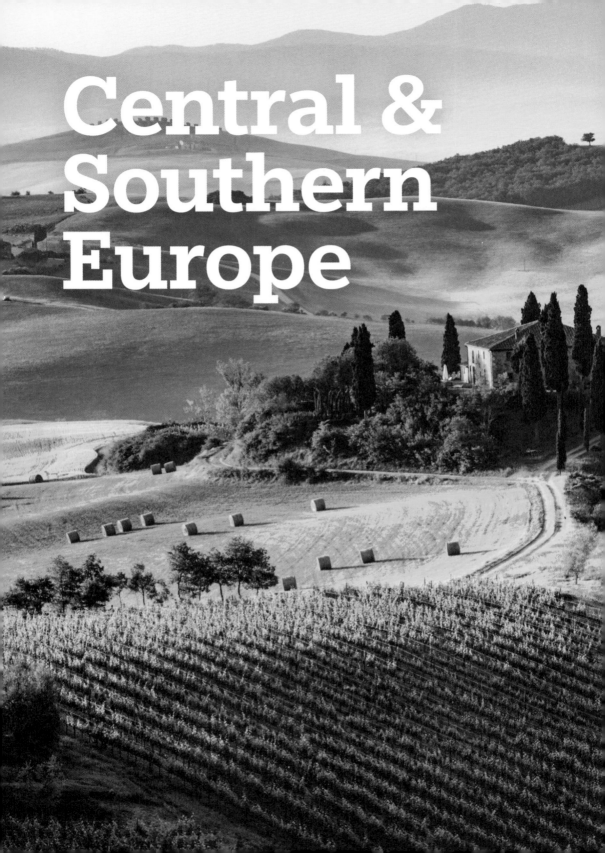

Central & Southern Europe

Austria

104 käsepäetzle
spaetzle with cheese

106 linzer biscuits

108 mohnkuchen
poppy seed cake

110 sachertorte
Austrian chocolate cake

Hungary

112 dobos torte
Hungarian layered cake

114 goulash
traditional Hungarian stew

Italy

116 calamaretti
baby squid stew

118 pasta con spinaci e pomodori
pasta with spinach & tomatoes

120 ravioli con pera e Gorgonzola
pear & Gorgonzola ravioli

122 risotto al nero di seppia
risotto with squid ink

124 goat's cheese polenta
with slow-roasted tomatoes & spinach

125 salame di cioccolato
chocolate salami

126 spaghetti
with courgettes, basil & Parmesan

käesespäetzle
spaetzle with cheese

Jacqueline Frisby, Eurotunnel's Flexiplus Lounge Manager, is from Austria and says this is her country's version of mac 'n' cheese. 'Although spaetzle are a type of soft egg noodle, they have never rivalled Italian pasta in popularity and are rarely seen outside southern Germany, Austria, Switzerland and Hungary. Spaetzle are delicious, though, so do try your hand at making them. They are a bit more challenging to master than ordinary pasta but well worth the effort.'

Preparation: 30 minutes, plus 1 hour standing • Cooking: about 15–20 minutes • Serves 4

ingredients

for the spaetzle

3 large eggs

175ml milk

1 tsp mustard

¼ tsp freshly grated nutmeg

375g strong white bread flour

200g grated hard cheese, eg Emmenthal, Gruyère, Appenzell

for the onions

75g butter

2 medium onions, peeled and sliced into thin rings

black mustard seeds, to garnish

method

To make the spaetzle, whisk the eggs together in a large mixing bowl and then whisk in the milk, mustard and nutmeg. Whisk in the flour – do this very gradually to prevent lumps from forming – and continue to whisk until you have a batter that is similar to a pancake batter but thicker. Cover the bowl with cling film and set aside in a cool place for 1 hour.

Now comes the tricky part for the novice spaetzle chef! Bring a large pan of salted water to the boil and push the batter straight into the water through a spaetzle maker, potato ricer, metal colander or a large mesh sieve. You need to push quite hard to get the thick batter through the holes and into the water and a flat spaetzle maker is the easiest tool for doing this, as it will sit on top of the pan and you can push the batter through with the scraper provided.

Bring the water in the pan back to the boil and as soon as the spaetzle float, drain them with a slotted spoon.

Layer up the spaetzle and grated cheese in a warm serving dish, finishing with a layer of cheese. Keep warm in a low oven.

To make the onion topping, melt the butter in a frying pan, add the onions and fry over a low heat until they are golden brown. Pile the onions on top of the spaetzle, sprinkle with black mustard seeds and serve accompanied with a salad or apple compote.

linzer biscuits

Linz is Austria's third largest city and home to the famous Linzertorte, a sweet tart made with almond pastry filled with jam and topped with a lattice crust. Served at Christmas time, the traditional filling for the tart in Austria was blackcurrant jam but once the recipe crossed the Atlantic, Americans decided they preferred raspberry. Linzer biscuits are smaller versions of the Linzertorte, the dough being rolled thinly, cut out using fancy cutters and sandwiched in pairs with jam. The top biscuit has small 'Linzer eye' cut outs to show the jam inside and while these were originally round, fancy shapes such as hearts have now become popular.

Preparation: 45 minutes, plus 1½ hours chilling • Cooking: 10–12 minutes • Makes about 20

ingredients

for the biscuit dough

300g plain flour

200g butter, chilled and cut into small dice

100g caster sugar

100g ground almonds or ground walnuts

½ tsp ground cinnamon

2 large egg yolks, beaten

1–2 tbsp milk

for the filling

apricot jam or redcurrant jelly

icing sugar, to dust

method

To make the biscuit dough, sieve the flour into a mixing bowl and rub in the butter until the texture is like fine breadcrumbs. Stir in the caster sugar, ground nuts and cinnamon and then add the egg yolks.

Bring all the ingredients together with your hand, adding enough milk to make a soft dough. Knead lightly until smooth, shape the dough into a flattened disc, wrap it in cling film and chill in the fridge for 1 hour.

Roll out the dough to 5mm thick between two sheets of baking parchment to prevent it sticking to the work surface or rolling pin. Cut out biscuits using different shaped cutters and then cut out smaller shapes from the centre of half the biscuits. Gather up any dough trimmings to re-roll and make more biscuits.

Lift the biscuits onto baking sheets lined with baking parchment and chill for 30 minutes.

Preheat the oven to 180°C (160°C fan)/Gas mark 4.

Bake the biscuits for about 10–12 minutes or until they are turning golden at the edges. Slide the biscuits off the baking sheets onto a wire rack to cool.

To fill, spread the plain biscuits with a little jam or jelly (if using redcurrant jelly, beat it first with a fork to make it soft enough to spread), then gently press biscuits of the same shape with the cut out centres on top. Store the biscuits in an airtight container and dust with icing sugar before serving.

mohnkuchen
poppy seed cake

Preparation: 1 hour, plus 30 minutes chilling • Cooking: 1 hour • Serves 8

ingredients

250g plain flour, plus extra for rolling out

1 tsp baking powder

1 egg

100g caster sugar

1 tsp vanilla extract or vanilla sugar

150g unsalted butter, diced & softened

350ml milk

120g caster sugar

1 tsp vanilla extract or vanilla sugar

pinch of ground cinnamon

½ tsp finely grated lemon zest

200g black poppy seeds

50g semolina

½ tsp rum

50g plain flour

½ tsp ground cinnamon

2 tbsp brown sugar

40g unsalted butter, diced & softened

icing or caster sugar for dusting

method

To make the pastry, sieve the flour and baking powder onto a board and make a well in the centre. Crack the egg into the well and add the sugar, vanilla and diced butter. Work the egg, sugar and butter together with a fork or your fingers and then mix in the flour and baking powder, kneading lightly to make a soft, smooth dough. Wrap in cling film and chill in the fridge for 30 minutes.

Roll out the pastry on a lightly floured board large enough to line the base and come about 5cm up the sides of a 20cm spring-spriclip tin. Return to the fridge while you make the filling.

To make the filling, bring 200ml of the milk, 100g of the sugar, the vanilla, cinnamon and lemon zest to the boil. Stir in the poppy seeds and leave to simmer, stirring occasionally, while you bring the remaining milk and sugar to the boil in a separate pan. Stir in the semolina until thickened and then stir the two mixtures together.

Finally stir in the rum.

To make the crumble topping, sieve the flour and cinnamon into a bowl. Stir in the sugar and gradually rub in the butter until the mixture resembles coarse breadcrumbs.

Preheat the oven to 180°C (160°fan)/Gas mark 4.

Spoon the poppy seed filling into the pastry case and cover with the crumble topping. Bake in the oven for about 1 hour or until the topping is golden.

Cool for about 15 minutes before removing from the tin. Serve dusted with icing or caster sugar.

Frequent Traveller, Bob Mason, has spent many weeks based at the Hotel Wienerhof in Trins, Gschnitzal, just south of Innsbruck, while leading walking and cross-country skiing holidays for a major travel company. 'One of my favourite recipes from the Tyrol is this unusual cake made by the hotel chef, Arno Uberganger,' says Bob.

sachertorte
Austrian chocolate cake

Created in 1832 by Franz Sacher, a 16-year-old apprentice chef at the court of Prince Metternich, his Sachertorte remains one of the world's most famous chocolate cakes. The original recipe is closely guarded by the bakers at the Hotel Sacher in Vienna, where it is kept locked away in the hotel's safe, but this version comes close both in texture and flavour.

Preparation: 1 hour, plus cooling and setting • Cooking: 50 minutes • Serves 10

ingredients

for the cake mixture

175g dark chocolate, chopped

150g butter, diced and softened

115g soft dark brown sugar

1 tsp vanilla extract

5 eggs, separated

4 tbsp plain flour

75g ground almonds

to decorate

4 tbsp apricot jam

1 tsp lemon juice

250g dark chocolate, chopped, plus extra for piping

125g good quality milk chocolate (see our tip)

300ml double cream

edible gold leaf

method

To make the cake mixture, grease a 23cm spring-clip tin and line the sides with baking parchment. Melt the chocolate in a bowl over a pan of hot water, without letting the bottom of the bowl touch the water, stirring until smooth. Set aside to cool.

Cream the butter, sugar and vanilla together until light and fluffy. Beat in the egg yolks one at a time until evenly mixed in, followed by the cooled chocolate, flour and ground almonds.

In a separate bowl, whisk the egg whites until standing in firm peaks. Beat 2 tablespoons of the whisked whites into the cake batter to soften it and then carefully fold in the rest using a large metal spoon, until evenly combined.

Preheat the oven to 180°C (160°C fan)/Gas mark 4. Pour the cake mixture into the tin and bake for 50 minutes or until a skewer pushed into the centre comes out clean. Leave the cake to cool in the tin for 15 minutes before turning it out onto a wire rack to cool completely.

To decorate the cake, warm the apricot jam with the lemon juice and then sieve to remove any large pieces of fruit. With the cake still sitting on the wire rack, brush the top and sides of it with the hot jam.

To make the icing, melt the dark and milk chocolate with the cream in a bowl over a pan of hot water, stirring until smooth. Spoon half into another bowl and chill until firm enough to spread over the top and sides of the cake, smoothing it in an even layer. Put a sheet of baking parchment under the wire rack to catch any drips. Re-melt the remaining chocolate icing by standing the bowl over hot water again and pour over the cake. So that it coats the cake smoothly and evenly, ease it down the sides by tilting the rack. Leave until the icing has set before decorating the top with tiny pieces of edible gold leaf (see our tip).

our tip

If the icing is made solely with dark chocolate that contains a high percentage of cocoa solids, it will be too strong for some tastes. Using a combination of dark and milk chocolate, gives a creamier, less bitter, result.

Sheets of edible gold leaf are available from larger supermarkets in the baking ingredients aisle. The foil sheets are very fine and will stick to your fingers and tear if you touch them. Pull off tiny pieces with 2 fine paintbrushes and place them directly on the cake.

dobos torte
Hungarian layered cake

This spectacular cake of wafer thin layers of sponge sandwiched with buttercream and topped with caramel, was created in 1884 by Hungarian confectioner Jozsef C. Dobos. He wanted a cake that customers could keep for longer than the pastries he baked and he achieved this by adding a caramel topping that prevented the sponge from drying out. It was an instant success, with Emperor Franz Joseph I and Empress Elisabeth among its early fans.

Preparation: 1 hour • Cooking: about 30 minutes, plus cooling and setting • Serves 8

ingredients

for the sponge layers

6 eggs

225g caster sugar

1 tsp vanilla extract

200g self-raising flour

for the chocolate buttercream

2 egg whites

125g icing sugar, sieved

225g unsalted butter, diced and softened

125g dark chocolate, melted and cooled

to decorate

75g granulated sugar

2 tbsp water

75g chopped toasted hazelnuts

method

To make the sponge layers, preheat the oven to 200°C (180°C fan)/ Gas mark 6. Draw 20cm circles on sheets of baking parchment and place on baking sheets – you should be able to make 7 layers from the quantity of cake mixture. Whisk together the eggs, sugar and vanilla until pale, thick and creamy. Sieve in the flour and lightly fold it in until combined. Spoon a little mixture onto the marked circles, spreading it thinly and evenly. Bake the layers in batches for 8–10 minutes or until they are golden and springy to the touch. As they come out of the oven, trim the edges neatly, peel off the baking parchment and cool the layers on a wire rack.

To make the chocolate buttercream, place a bowl over a pan of simmering water, add the egg whites and icing sugar and whisk until the whites are standing in soft peaks. In another bowl, beat the butter until soft and creamy and then whisk in the egg whites a little at a time. Stir in the melted chocolate until evenly combined.

To make the caramel, place one sponge layer upside down on a sheet of baking parchment. Dissolve the granulated sugar in the water over a gentle heat and then boil the syrup to a golden caramel – don't let the caramel become too brown as it will continue to darken after you've removed it from the heat. Leave the caramel to cool for a couple of minutes before pouring it over the sponge layer. When the caramel starts to set but is not yet hard, cut it into 8 wedges with an oiled knife. When hard, snip off any excess caramel with scissors to neaten the edges.

To assemble the cake, sandwich the plain sponge layers with some of the buttercream. Spread more buttercream around the sides of the cake and press on the chopped hazelnuts. Pipe or spoon rosettes of the remaining buttercream on top of the cake and position the caramel triangles between them at an angle.

goulash
traditional Hungarian stew

Isabelle Dubruille, Eurotunnel's Project Manager, learnt how to prepare this traditional Hungarian stew from her grandmother. 'I've now taught my two 25-year-old daughters how to make it and I'm delighted to report their boyfriends love it too!' says Isabelle proudly. 'My grandmother didn't add red peppers to her goulash but I've added them here as they are so colourful and, of course, she only ever used genuine Hungarian paprika.'

Preparation: 25 minutes • Cooking: 1¾–2¼ hours • Serves 6

ingredients

3 tbsp oil

700g chuck or braising steak, cut into 2cm cubes

2 tbsp plain flour

3 large onions, peeled and chopped

3 tbsp Hungarian paprika

1 tsp cayenne

2 red peppers, deseeded and chopped

400g can chopped tomatoes

2 tbsp tomato purée

500ml beef stock

chopped fresh parsley, to serve

salt and pepper

method

Preheat the oven to 170°C (150°C fan)/Gas mark 3. Heat the oil in a large flameproof casserole. Toss the cubes of meat in the flour and brown in batches in the hot oil, removing them from the pan as they brown.

When all the steak has been browned, add the onions to the casserole and fry over a low heat until the onions are soft but not browned.

Add the paprika and cayenne, fry for 1 minute and then add the peppers, tomatoes, tomato purée and stock. Bring to the boil and season lightly with salt and pepper.

Cover the casserole with foil and a lid and cook in the oven for 1½–2 hours or until the meat is very tender. Serve sprinkled with chopped parsley and accompany with rice.

calamaretti
baby squid stew

'I spend several months of the year in Calabria, southern Italy, and often take the ferry over to Messina in Sicily,' says Frequent Traveller, Jane Wagner. 'Living on the coast I can buy plenty of fish straight from the sea and some catches and species are very local indeed. I'm now 83 but continue to drive regularly all the way from London to the Mediterranean. I married a Frenchman and had a varied professional career working as a linguist, including positions with the UK civil service, the UN in West Africa and the UN World Food programme in Rome.'

Preparation: 15 minutes • Cooking: 45 minutes • Serves 2

ingredients

2 tbsp olive oil

2–3 parsley sprigs, finely chopped, plus extra to serve

1 large garlic clove, peeled and finely chopped

3 anchovy fillets preserved in oil, or salted anchovies rinsed and chopped

300g small squid, cleaned and cut into bite-size pieces

125ml dry white wine

200g tomatoes, peeled and deseeded (or use canned ones)

1 bird's eye chilli, other small red chilli or a pinch of dried chilli flakes

50g fresh or frozen peas (optional)

salt

method

Heat the oil in a heavy pan with a lid, such as a cast iron one, add the chopped parsley sprigs and garlic and sweat over a medium heat until the garlic is softened but not browned. Stir in the anchovies and cook until they dissolve. Add the squid, stir and let it absorb the other flavours for 2 minutes over a medium-low heat.

Pour in the wine and leave it to evaporate without increasing the heat. Add the tomatoes, chilli, peas (if using) and season with a pinch of salt. Cover the pan and cook over a low heat for about 30 minutes, checking occasionally to make sure the stew is not too dry – add a little warm water if necessary.

Serve with extra chopped parsley sprinkled over and accompanied with plain boiled rice.

pasta con spinaci e pomodori
pasta with spinach & tomatoes

'I was given this recipe by an Italian friend who I met in England but has now moved back to Italy to be a film critic,' says Jan Kuba, System Specialist at Eurotunnel. 'I love the recipe because it's light, quick and easy to make and, if you use whole wheat pasta as an alternative to ordinary pasta, it's an even healthier dish.'

Preparation: 15 minutes • Cooking: 25 minutes • Serves 2–3

ingredients

2 tbsp olive oil

1 onion, peeled and finely chopped

400g frozen spinach

140g–210g dried pasta spirals (70g per person)

4 tomatoes, peeled if preferred

2–4 garlic cloves, according to taste, peeled and crushed

a small handful of fresh basil leaves

125g mozzarella cheese, cut into 2cm cubes

grated Parmesan cheese, to serve

salt and pepper

method

Heat the oil in a large, deep frying pan that has a lid and fry the onion over a low heat until it is softened and lightly coloured. Add the spinach, cover the pan and, when it has defrosted, remove the lid and let the mixture bubble so the excess liquid can evaporate.

Bring a large pan of boiling salted water to the boil, add the pasta and cook according to the packet instructions.

Meanwhile, chop the tomatoes into small chunks and stir into the spinach. Season with salt and pepper, cover the pan and cook until the tomatoes are soft and pulpy. Add the garlic and basil leaves and leave to simmer until the pasta is ready.

Drain the pasta and stir gently into the spinach mixture so as not to break up the spirals. Add the cubes of mozzarella and transfer to hot serving plates. Sprinkle with grated Parmesan and garnish with extra basil leaves.

ravioli con pera e Gorgonzola
pear & Gorgonzola ravioli

Preparation: 1 hour, plus 1 hour resting • Cooking: 15 minutes • Serves 4 – as a starter

ingredients

for the pasta dough

140g Italian '00' flour or plain flour

1 whole egg

1 egg yolk

for the filling

2 ripe Williams or Packham pears, 230g peeled and cored weight

110g unsalted butter

125g Gorgonzola cheese

2 tbsp double cream

semolina flour, for dusting

sea salt and freshly ground black pepper

to serve

sea salt flakes

toasted pine kernels, optional

method

To make the pasta dough, pulse the flour in a food processor for a few seconds. Add the egg and egg yolk and process for 2–3 minutes until the mixture resembles fine breadcrumbs – it shouldn't be dusty, nor a big, gooey ball. Tip out the dough onto a work surface and knead into a ball for 1 minute, by which time the dough should be quite stiff. Wrap in cling film and leave to rest in a cool place for 1 hour.

Meanwhile, make the filling. Chop the pears into small dice. Heat 10g of the butter in a small pan over a medium heat, add the pears and cook for about 5 minutes until softened. Remove from the heat and leave to cool. Put the Gorgonzola and cream in a mini-processor and process until smooth. Mix with the pears and season with salt and pepper.

Cut the pasta dough in half and flatten each with a rolling pin until about 5mm thick. Working with one piece at a time, fold the dough over and pass it through a pasta machine at its widest setting, refolding and rolling 7 times without changing the setting until the dough is rectangular and measures about 7.5cm × 18cm. It is important to work the dough until it is nice and shiny as this gives it its 'al dente' texture. Repeat with the second piece of dough.

Start with the pasta machine on its widest setting and pass one sheet of dough through, without folding it this time, decreasing the setting each time, until you reach the penultimate setting for ravioli. Place heaped teaspoons of the filling on half the pasta sheet, dampen the edges around each and fold the other half of the dough over. Seal around each heap of filling with your fingers, taking care not to trap any air inside. Cut out circles with a ravioli or fluted cutter and lightly dust the parcels with semolina. Keep them covered with a clean tea towel while you make more ravioli with the other sheet of pasta.

Cook the ravioli for 6–7 minutes in a large pan of well-salted water. While the ravioli parcels are cooking, heat the remaining 100g butter in a large frying pan until melted. Drain the cooked ravioli, add to the pan and toss for 1–2 minutes until coated with the butter. Serve at once with black pepper grated over and sprinkled with sea salt flakes. Top with toasted pine kernels, if wished.

Brand Executive, Suzanne Winham, tells us she travelled with Eurotunnel a few years ago to the beautiful resort of Malcesine on the eastern shore of Lake Garda. 'The holiday was wonderful,' remembers Suzanne,' and one of the highlights was this delicious dish of ravioli filled with pear and Gorgonzola.'

risotto al nero di seppia
risotto with squid ink

Venice's chefs usually make this classic risotto with cuttlefish as these cephalopods contain more ink than smaller squid, giving the finished dish its dramatic, jet-black appearance. Cuttlefish ink also imbues the rice with the briny flavour of the sea and this contrasts beautifully with the sweetness of the cuttlefish. Back home, it's not easy to track down cuttlefish that still contain their ink but ready-prepared squid and small plastic sachets of ink are more widely available. The resulting risotto won't be as black and shiny as a true Venetian original but it will still taste delicious.

Preparation: 15 minutes • Cooking: about 1 hour • Serves 2

ingredients

3 tbsp extra virgin olive oil

1 medium onion, peeled and finely chopped

1 garlic clove, peeled and finely chopped

200g squid, cleaned and cut into rings or bite-size pieces

90ml dry white wine

900ml hot fish stock

2 tsp tomato purée

175g carnaroli risotto rice

4g sachet of squid ink

25g butter

2 tbsp finely chopped fresh parsley

salt and freshly ground black pepper

method

Heat 2 tablespoons of the oil in a saucepan over a medium heat and cook the onion until softened but not browned. Add the garlic, fry for 1 minute and then add the squid. Cook for 1 minute and then add 4 tablespoons of the wine, 150ml of the stock and the tomato purée. Cover and simmer gently over a very low heat for 30 minutes, stirring from time to time, or until the squid is very tender, adding a little water if necessary. Remove from the heat, lift out the squid from its cooking liquid with a draining spoon and set aside, reserving the cooking liquid.

Heat the remaining stock in a saucepan until simmering. Heat the rest of the oil in a large, deep frying pan, add the rice and cook for 2 minutes until the grains are opaque, stirring occasionally. Add the rest of the wine, let this evaporate and then add a ladleful of the hot stock. Wait for the rice to absorb the stock before adding another a ladleful, stirring frequently to stop the rice sticking.

Continue adding the stock in this way and when about half of it has been added and absorbed by the rice, stir in three quarters of the squid, its cooking juices and the squid ink. Keep the rest of the squid warm in a low oven. Season the risotto and then continue adding more stock until the rice is tender but still has a little bite. Remove the pan from the heat and stir in the butter until it has melted.

Serve the risotto straight away, topped with the remaining squid and sprinkled with the chopped parsley.

goat's cheese polenta
with slow-roasted tomatoes & spinach

Polenta is made by grinding corn to a meal and it is one of those ingredients that people either love or hate. It can be served in two ways and the first, where the cooked polenta is left to go cold and become solid, before it is sliced and reheated on a griddle, probably explains why so many people dislike it. However, in this recipe, the polenta is served hot, as soon as it is cooked, so it remains soft with a light, fluffy texture. Goat's cheese is stirred in at the end to add extra flavour and creaminess so, if you think polenta is not for you, this recipe might just change your mind.

Preparation: 15 minutes • Cooking: about 15 minutes • Serves 4

ingredients

200g cherry tomatoes on the vine

2 garlic cloves, peeled and chopped

leaves from 4 sprigs of fresh thyme

3 tbsp balsamic vinegar

2 tbsp olive oil

600ml milk and water mixed, in equal quantities

100g quick cook polenta

125g goat's cheese, chopped or crumbled

100g baby spinach leaves

salt and pepper

method

Preheat the oven to 200°C (180°C fan)/Gas mark 6. Divide the tomatoes into small sprigs and spread them out in a shallow roasting tin. Sprinkle over the garlic and thyme and drizzle with the vinegar and oil. Season and roast for 15 minutes or until the tomato skins are starting to split.

Meanwhile, bring the milk and water to the boil in a large saucepan and whisk in the polenta until smooth and there are no lumps. Simmer for 15 minutes or until the polenta is thick, has absorbed the milk and water and is coming away from the sides of the pan. Stir in the goat's cheese until it has melted.

Rinse the spinach leaves under cold water and put in a pan with just the rinsing water on the leaves. Place the pan over a medium heat, cover with a lid and cook the spinach for 3–4 minutes or until it has wilted. Serve the polenta as soon as it is ready, accompanied with the roasted tomatoes and spinach.

Italy

salame di cioccolato
chocolate salami

Nelly Burnier-Framboret, who is one of our Call Centre Agents, says she can't resist this unusual chocolate and nut treat. 'It's really easy to make and once the 'salami' has been rolled in icing sugar and tied up with thin string, it looks just like the real thing! It's delicious cut into thin slices and served with after dinner coffee.'

Preparation: 30 minutes, plus chilling • Makes 3 x 20cm 'salamis'

ingredients

225g dark chocolate, chopped

100g unsalted butter, diced

75g soft dark brown sugar

1 tbsp cocoa powder

2 egg yolks

2 tbsp Tia Maria or strong black coffee

175g crisp amaretti biscuits

50g whole blanched almonds, chopped

50g hazelnuts, chopped

25g pistachios, chopped

icing sugar, for dusting

method

Put the chopped chocolate, butter, sugar, cocoa powder, egg yolks and Tia Maria or coffee in a saucepan over a low heat, stirring until the chocolate, butter and sugar have melted, the ingredients are evenly combined and you have a smooth mixture.

Crush or chop the amaretti into coarse crumbs and stir into the melted mixture with the nuts.

Chill in the fridge for 30 minutes or until the mixture has firmed up but is not too hard to be moulded.

Divide the mixture into three and spoon each onto a sheet of cling film or baking parchment. Shape into long, thin logs, roll the cling film or parchment around the logs and twist the ends to seal. Chill in the fridge for 4 hours or until firm.

Unwrap the logs, roll the salami in icing sugar and, if wished, tie it up with knotted thin string like real salami.

When ready to serve, remove from the fridge and cut into thin slices with a sharp knife.

spaghetti
with courgettes, basil & Parmesan

British-born celebrity chef, Theo Randall, specialises in cooking Italian cuisine and he won a Michelin Star for his innovative dishes at London's River Café. A frequent Eurotunnel traveller, he has now opened his own eponymous restaurant at the InterContinental Hotel in Park Lane, voted one of the top Italian restaurants in the country. We were delighted when Theo agreed to share one of his favourite pasta recipes with us.

Preparation: 15 minutes • Cooking: about 30 minutes • Serves 4 – as a starter

ingredients

4 tbsp olive oil

2 medium white onions, peeled and thinly sliced

4 courgettes, sliced across into 1cm rounds

8 basil leaves

300g spaghetti

4 courgette flowers, ripped into strips

2 egg yolks

100g grated Parmesan cheese, plus extra to serve

salt and freshly ground black pepper

method

Heat 2 tablespoons of the olive oil in a pan, add the sliced onions and fry over a very low heat for 20 minutes until the onions are soft but not coloured.

At the same time, heat the remaining oil in a large frying pan and fry the courgettes gently for 20 minutes until soft. Add the basil leaves so the courgettes absorb the flavour of the basil. Season and take the pan off the heat, leaving the courgettes and basil in the pan.

Bring a large saucepan of salted water to the boil, add the spaghetti and cook for 2 minutes less than the packet instructions. Lift the spaghetti out of the pan with a pair of tongs, add to the frying pan with the courgettes and 1 ladle of the pasta cooking water.

Put the frying pan back on the hob and add the onions and courgette flowers to the spaghetti. Cook for a couple of minutes.

Beat the egg yolks and Parmesan together in a bowl and pour into the pan. Toss well with the spaghetti and add a little more pasta water so it remains really creamy.

Serve in hot bowls with black pepper grated over and a little extra grated Parmesan on the side.

dietary tip Gluten-free or whole wheat spaghetti can be used if you wish.

Drinks

Italy

130 hugo cocktail

131 bellini cocktail

France

132 champagne soup

133 kir royale
kir

Germany

134 eiskaffee
traditional German iced coffee

Austria

135 glühwein
traditional Austrian mulled wine

hugo cocktail

Emma Daniels is Eurotunnel's Social Media & Content Executive and writes her own travel and lifestyle blog. She explains how she was introduced to this cocktail when she was visiting a German friend in Regensburg. 'I'd met the friend travelling,' says Emma, 'and her step-dad was kind enough to give us a tour of the city. After an awful lot of walking, we sat down in a bar opposite the cathedral and I assumed we'd have a beer but instead this Prosecco cocktail arrived. As the temperature at the time was over 30 degrees centigrade, it was really welcome as it was so refreshing!'

Preparation: 5 minutes • Serves 4

ingredients

ice cubes

fresh mint leaves

8 tbsp elderflower cordial

100ml soda water

200ml Prosecco

1 lime, sliced

method

Put 3 or 4 ice cubes in each glass and add some small fresh mint leaves.

Divide the elderflower cordial and soda water between the glasses and top up with the Prosecco.

Decorate with lime slices and serve at once.

did you know?

This Italian elderflower spritz, called 'Ugo' in Italy, was only invented around 10 years ago but it has rapidly become very popular, especially when the weather is hot. However, its Italian origins are hotly disputed by Austrians, who believe it was created in the Tyrol; Hugo deriving from the old high German word 'hugu', meaning 'heart, mind and spirit'.

bellini cocktail

This celebrated cocktail is a favourite with Brand Executive, Suzanne Winham, who says it has an interesting history. 'After seeing an exhibition of the paintings of Venetian Renaissance artist, Giovanni Bellini, Giuseppe Cipriani, the bartender of the legendary Harry's Bar in Venice, created this champagne and peach juice cocktail as its colour reminded Cipriani of Bellini's paintings.' A true Bellini is made using fresh white peaches but as their season is only short, most amateur bartenders resort to using the more readily-available yellow-fleshed fruit – unless, of course, they've stocked their freezer with enough white peach purée to see them through the year.

Preparation: 10 minutes • Serves 2

ingredients

2 small or 1 large white peach

2 tsp freshly-squeezed lemon juice

2 tbsp freshly-squeezed orange juice

about 300ml Prosecco

peach slices, to serve

method

Put the peaches in a bowl and pour over boiling water to cover them. Leave for 1–2 minutes, then drain and cool under cold water. Nick the skin in several places with the point of a sharp knife and peel it off.

Halve and stone the peaches, chop the flesh and blend with the lemon juice and orange juice until smooth.

One quarter fill well-chilled champagne flutes with the peach purée (any left over can be frozen for another occasion) and top up with Prosecco. Decorate the glasses with a peach slice.

France

champagne soup

'No Eurotunnel cook book would be complete without at least one of France's famous champagne cocktails,' says Marketing Communications Executive, Rose Joyner, 'and this is definitely one of my favourites. If you've something special to celebrate, this extra special 'soup' can be relied on to get your guests in the party mood!'

Preparation: 5 minutes, plus overnight chilling • Serves 8–10

ingredients

100ml Cointreau

3 tbsp sugar syrup

100ml lemon juice

ice cubes

1 bottle of champagne
(or you could use sparkling wine)

lemon wedges, to serve

method

Pour the Cointreau, sugar syrup and lemon juice into a jug and chill in the fridge overnight to allow the flavours to mingle and develop.

Put a couple of ice cubes into each champagne glass – 'I prefer to use traditional coupes rather than more modern flutes,' says Rose – pour in the Cointreau mixture and top up with champagne (or sparkling wine).

Drop a small wedge of lemon into each glass and serve without delay.

kir royale & kir

'My Dad travels to France frequently,'
says Emma Daniels, Eurotunnel's Social Media
and Content Executive, 'so when I went to Nantes
on my way to a French music festival with a bunch
of friends in tow, he recommended we try this
classic French cocktail. That evening, before heading
to the festival campsite the next day, we went to a
bar and ordered a kir royale. The barman looked
both surprised and delighted so he must have
either been impressed with our knowledge of local
culture or our knowledge of cocktails!'

Preparation: 5 minutes • Serves 1

kir royale

ingredients

1 tbsp Crème de Cassis, Crème de Framboise, Crème de Fraise
des Bois or another fruit liqueur

125ml champagne or French sparkling wine

sprig of blackcurrants, a raspberry or a few wild strawberries,
depending on the fruit liqueur you used

method

Spoon the fruit liqueur into a champagne flute and top up with
the champagne or sparkling wine. Decorate with fresh fruit to
match the fruit liqueur you have added.

kir

ingredients

1 tbsp Crème de Cassis, Crème de Framboise, Crème de Fraise
des Bois or another fruit liqueur

125ml dry white wine, well chilled

method

Spoon the fruit liqueur into a stemmed wine glass and top up
with the white wine. As with a kir royale, you can decorate the
drink with fresh fruit to match the fruit liqueur you have added.

eiskaffee
traditional German iced coffee

Popular in summer, not just at pavement cafés in Germany but in traditional coffee houses in Austria as well, this is a great way to cool down on a hot day. The basic recipe is just ice cream and cold coffee, topped with whipped cream, but, as you can imagine, there are lots of variations. Some cafés add evaporated milk, others sweeten the cream and the strength of the coffee can be varied, depending on how much of a caffeine hit the customer needs.

Preparation: 5 minutes • Serves 1

ingredients

2 scoops of vanilla, coffee or chocolate ice cream

150ml cold strong black coffee, chilled

3 tbsp whipped cream

chocolate shavings or grated chocolate, to serve

method

Put the scoops of ice cream into a tall glass.

Pour over the coffee and top with the whipped cream.

Serve immediately with chocolate shavings or grated chocolate sprinkled over.

Austria

glühwein
traditional Austrian mulled wine

'One of my fondest memories is going to Christmas markets with my family when I was growing up in Germany and the warm, spicy aroma of glühwein that filled the air,' says Monique Dixon – Data Executive at Eurotunnel. 'Nowadays I love making it for friends and family in the UK as, not only does it give me the chance to introduce them to this traditional festive drink, but it also reminds me of those trips to the market at Christmas time.'

Preparation: 10 minutes • Cooking: 25 minutes • Serves 10

ingredients

2 oranges

1 lemon, sliced

6 whole cloves

500ml water

150g granulated or caster sugar

2 cinnamon sticks

2 star anise

2 bottles of red wine

to serve

1 orange, studded with cloves and cut into small pieces

method

Peel the zest from the oranges using a vegetable peeler but leaving behind the white pith. Put the strips of zest into a large saucepan, squeeze in the juice from the oranges and add the lemon slices, cloves, water and sugar.

Stir over a low heat until the sugar has dissolved. Add the cinnamon sticks and star anise and bring to the boil. Simmer for 1 minute.

Pour in the wine and immediately reduce the heat to very low. Leave to simmer gently for 20 minutes, without letting the liquid boil.

Strain the glühwein and serve warm in mugs or heatproof glasses, adding a small chunk of orange studded with cloves to each serving.

meet our canine travellers

dog biscuits

Eurotunnel's Campaigns Manager, Fiona Robbins, has lived with dogs since she was young. 'I currently have six small dogs, all of which travel with us,' says Fiona. 'They sit on the back seat strapped to a seatbelt and, as well as water, we make sure they have some treats to keep them happy. These dog biscuits are a great favourite and they'll sniff them out with great excitement and vigorous tail wagging even before we've set off.'

Preparation: 15 minutes, plus chilling • Cooking: 30 minutes
Makes about 16, depending on size of cutters used

ingredients

4 tbsp warm water

80g smooth or crunchy peanut butter (choose a brand that is unsweetened)

200g plain flour

75g porridge oats

40g grated Parmesan cheese

1 egg, beaten

method

In a mixing bowl, stir the warm water into the peanut butter until smooth. Sieve in the flour and stir in with the oats and cheese until all the ingredients are evenly combined.

Mix in the beaten egg to make a dough and knead for 1–2 minutes.

Roll out the dough 1½cm thick and cut out biscuits. Line a baking sheet with baking parchment, lift the biscuits onto it and chill in the fridge for 30 minutes to firm them up.

Preheat the oven to 180°C (160°C fan)/Gas mark 4 and bake the biscuits for 30 minutes or until golden brown and crisp.

Well, there you are.
69 recipes from 22 countries, covering every course and palate.

Recipes galore to take your friends, family and even Fido on a European taste adventure.

The Europhile's Cookbook has been 25 years in the making, meaning there are so many people we'd like to thank for their time, talent and travels.

Firstly, to all those who have sent us the recipes they've discovered and had handed down to them – thank you for sharing your dishes with us and with all those who read this book. Every recipe has a story behind it and we've been truly humbled by the tales you've shared.

We'd also like to thank every one of our customers who has travelled with us – whether you've contributed to this book or not, we've been proud to share a piece of your journey with you and hope we've helped you bring back plenty of wonderful memories (and maybe a new favourite dish, snack or treat too).

While there's not enough room to mention everyone individually, there are a few people in particular we'd like to extend a special thank you to: Two-time World's Strongest Man, Olympian and loyal customer, Geoff Capes, for his Winter Belly Warmer. Michelin Star – winning chef and master of Italian cuisine, Theo Randall, for his spaghetti and Parmesan dish. And Paul Holt, who has not only been the ranger at Samphire Hoe since 1998, but provided a delicious recipe for this book (samphire included, naturally). Thank you to you all.

A final thanks goes to you for reading this cook book. We hope in years to come it's covered in fingerprints, splodges and splashes from all the use it gets – and hope that what you create helps you travel without even leaving the house.

share your creations

 @leshuttle

 eurotunnelleshuttle

 @LeShuttle

merci
thank you
grazie mille
köszönöm
gracias
danke

The Europhile's Cookbook
index

A

Aberdeen butteries (Rowies)	24
Aioli	95
Albondigas (Spanish meatballs)	96
Arroz de marisco (Shellfish with rice)	92
Austria: drinks	135
Austrian chocolate cake (Sachertorte)	110
Austria: recipes	104-110
A winter belly warmer (Traditional Lincolnshire meat dish)	15

B

Baby squid stew (Calamaretti)	116
Baklava	72
Bara brith (Welsh 'mottled or speckled bread')	26
Barszcz (Beetroot soup)	76
Beef	
Albondigas (Spanish meatballs)	96
Bitterballen (Dutch meatballs)	62
Goulash (Traditional Hungarian stew)	114
Sarma (Stuffed cabbage)	82
Steak & ale pies	16
Stoofvlees huisbereld met vleteren alt (Belgian beef stew)	56
Beetroot soup (Barszcz)	76
Belgian beef stew (Stoofvlees huisbereld met vleteren alt)	56
Belgium: recipes	54-56
Bellini cocktail	131
Benelux & Scandinavia: recipes	54-66
Bitterballen (Dutch meatballs)	62
Bread, Biscuits & Cakes	
Baklava	72
Bara brith (Welsh 'mottled or speckled bread')	26
Charlotte aux fraises (Strawberry Charlotte)	36
Dobos torte (Hungarian layered cake)	112
Dutch apple pie with a twist	58
Galette des rois (Kings' cake)	40
Lake Bled cream cake	86
Linzer biscuits	106
Mohnkuchen (Poppy seed cake)	108
Pastéis de nata (Portuguese custard tarts)	90
Sachertorte (Austrian chocolate cake)	110
Saint Nicolas biscuits (Traditional Christmas market biscuits)	30
Salame di cioccolato (Chocolate salami)	125
Sour cherry cake	78
British Isles: recipes	14-26

C

Calamaretti (Baby squid stew)	116
Cassoulet (Slow-cooked sausage & bean stew)	44
Central & Southern Europe: recipes	104-126
Champagne soup	132
Charlotte aux fraises (Strawberry Charlotte)	36
Cheese	
Crumbed Reblochon & salad board	48
Goat's cheese polenta with slow-roasted tomatoes & spinach	124
Käesespäetzle (Spaetzle with cheese)	104
Ravioli con pera e Gorgonzola (Pear & Gorgonzola ravioli)	120
Tartiflette (French-style cheesy potato bake)	33
Watermelon & feta salad	71
Zeljanica (filo pastry pie with spinach)	84
Chicken	
Jollof rice (West African one pot rice dish)	49
Spanish chicken with chorizo, peppers & olives	100
Chocolate salami (Salame di cioccolato) 125	
Cocktails	
Bellini	131
Champagne soup	132
Hugo	130
Kir royale & kir	133
Creamy fish stew (Waterzooi)	54
Croatia: recipe	70
Crumbed Reblochon & salad board	48
Crunchy cream puffs with Kirsch hot chocolate	433

D

Dandelion bud 'capers'	41
Dobos torte (Hungarian layered cake)	112
Dog biscuits	137
Drinks	130-135
Bellini cocktail	131
Champagne soup	132
Eiskaffee (Traditional German iced coffee)	134
Glühwein (Traditional Austrian mulled wine)	135
Hugo cocktail	130
Kir royale & kir	133
Kirsch hot chocolate	42
Dutch apple pie with a twist	58
Dutch carrot soup (Newspaper soup)	64
Dutch meatballs (Bitterballen)	62

E

Eiskaffee (Traditional German iced coffee) — 134
England: recipes — 14-21

F

Filo pastry pie with spinach (Zeljanica) — 84
Fish & seafood
   Arroz de marisco (Shellfish with rice) — 92
   Calamaretti (Baby squid stew) — 116
   Gravadlax with dill & mustard sauce — 66
   Oysters grilled with garlic, chilli & cream — 22
   Pan-fried hake with samphire — 18
   Salmon with grapes, prawns & parsley sauce — 20
   Scallops baked in the shell with a mousseline sauce — 34
   Waterzooi (Creamy fish stew) — 54
   Zoute haring (Salted pickled herrings) — 60
France: drinks — 132-133
France: recipes — 30-50
French-style cheesy potato bake (Tartiflette) — 33

G

Galette des rois (Kings' cake) — 40
Germany: drinks — 134
Glühwein (Traditional Austrian mulled wine) — 135
Goat's cheese polenta with
slow-roasted tomatoes & spinach — 124
Goulash (Traditional Hungarian stew) — 114
Gravadlax with dill & mustard sauce — 66
Greece: recipes — 71-74
Griddled potato wedges (Potato farls) — 23

H

Hugo cocktail — 130
Hungarian layered cake (Dobos torte) — 112
Hungary: recipes — 112-114

I

Ireland: recipe — 23
Italy: drinks — 130-131
Italy: recipes — 116-126

J

Jollof rice (West African one pot rice dish) — 49

K

Käesespäetzle (Spaetzle with cheese) — 104
Kings' cake (Galette des rois) — 40
Kir royale & kir — 133
Kirsch hot chocolate with crunchy
cream puffs (Le roustintin avec le craquelin) — 42

L

Lake Bled cream cake — 86
Lamb, chick pea & merguez tagine — 50
Lamb stifado (Lamb stewed with onions & red wine) — 74
Le roustintin avec le craquelin
(Kirsch hot chocolate with crunchy cream puffs) — 42
Linzer biscuits — 106

M

Mohnkuchen — 108

N

Netherlands: recipes — 58-64
Newspaper soup (Dutch carrot soup) — 64
North Africa: recipe — 50

O

Oysters grilled with garlic, chilli & cream — 22

P

Panettone pudding with mincemeat & apricots — 14
Pan-fried hake with samphire — 18
Pasta
   Käesespäetzle (Spaetzle with cheese) — 104
   Pasta con spinaci e pomodori
   (Pasta with spinach & tomatoes) — 118
   Ravioli con pera e Gorgonzola
   (Pear & Gorgonzola ravioli) — 120
   Spaghetti with courgettes, basil & Parmesan — 126
Pasta con spinaci e pomodori
(Pasta with spinach & tomatoes) — 118
Pasta with spinach & tomatoes
(Pasta con spinaci e pomodori) — 118
Pastéis de nata (Portuguese custard tarts) — 90
Patatas bravas — 95
Pear & Gorgonzola ravioli
(ravioli con pera e Gorgonzola) — 120
Pies
   Dutch apple pie with a twist — 58
   Steak & ale pies — 16
   Tarte Porteloise — 38
   Zeljanica (Filo pastry pie with spinach) — 84
Pimientos de padrón — 98
Plum dumplings — 70
Poland: recipe — 76
Poppy seed cake (Mohnkuchen) — 108
Porc à la Normande (Normandy pork) — 32
Pork
   Albondigas (Spanish meatballs) — 96
   A winter belly warmer
   (Traditional Lincolnshire meat dish) — 15
   Cassoulet (Slow-cooked sausage & bean stew) — 44

Porc à la Normande (Normandy pork) 32
Sarma (Stuffed cabbage) 82
Portugal: recipes 90-92
Portuguese custard tarts (Pastéis de nata) 90

Potatoes
Patatas bravas 95
Plum dumplings 70
Potato farls (Griddled potato wedges) 23
Spring potato salad 80
Tartiflette (French-style cheesy potato bake) 33
Tortilla Española 94
Potato farls (Griddled potato wedges) 23

R

Ravioli con pera e Gorgonzola
(Pear & Gorgonzola ravioli) 120

Rice
Arroz de marisco (Shellfish with rice) 92
Jollof rice (West African one pot rice dish) 49
Risotto al nero di seppia (Risotto with squid ink) 122
Risotto al nero di seppia (Risotto with squid ink) 122
Risotto with squid ink (Risotto al nero di sepia) 122
Romania: recipes 78-80
Rowies (Aberdeen butteries) 24

S

Sachertorte (Austrian chocolate cake) 110
Saint Nicolas biscuits
(Traditional Christmas market biscuits) 30

Salads
Salad board & crumbed Reblochon 48
Spring potato salad 80
Watermelon & feta salad 71
Salame di cioccolato (Chocolate salami) 125
Salmon with grapes, prawns & parsley sauce 20
Salted pickled herrings (Zoute haring) 60
Sarma (Stuffed cabbage) 82

Sauces
Aioli 95
Dill & mustard 66
Garlic, chilli & cream 22
Mousseline 34
Parsley 20
Tomato 96
Scallops baked in the shell with a mousseline sauce 34
Scandinavia: recipe 66
Scotland: recipe 24
Serbia: recipes 82-84
Shellfish with rice (Arroz de marisco) 92
Sicily: recipe 116
Slovenia: recipe 86
Slow-cooked sausage & bean stew (Cassoulet) 44
Soupe au pistou (Le pistou soup) 46

Soups
Barszcz (Beetroot soup) 76
Newspaper soup (Dutch carrot soup) 64
Soupe au pistou (Le pistou soup) 46
Sour cherry cake 78
South-East Europe: recipes 70-86
Spaetzle with cheese (Käesespäetzle) 104
Spaghetti with courgettes, basil & Parmesan 126
Spain & Portugal: recipes 90-100
Spain: recipes 94-100
Spanish chicken with chorizo, peppers & olives 100
Spanish meatballs (Albondigas) 96
Spring potato salad 80
Steak & ale pies 16

Stews
Calamaretti (Baby squid stew) 116
Cassoulet (Slow-cooked sausage & bean stew) 44
Goulash (Traditional Hungarian stew) 114
Jollof rice (West African one pot rice dish) 49
Lamb stifado (Lamb stewed with onions & red wine) 74
Stoofvlees huisbereld met vleteren alt
(Belgian beef stew) 56
Waterzooi (Creamy fish stew) 54
Strawberry Charlotte (Charlotte aux fraises) 36
Stuffed cabbage (Sarma) 82

T

Tapas 94
Tarte Porteloise 38
Tartiflette (French-style cheesy potato bake) 33
Tortilla Española 94
Traditional Austrian mulled wine (Glühwein) 135
Traditional Christmas market biscuits
(Saint Nicolas biscuits) 30
Traditional German iced coffee (Eiskaffee) 134
Traditional Hungarian stew (Goulash) 114
Traditional Lincolnshire meat dish
(A winter belly warmer) 15

W

Wales: recipe 26
Watermelon & feta salad 71
Waterzooi (Creamy fish stew) 54
Welsh 'mottled or speckled bread' (Bara brith) 26
West African one pot rice dish (Jollof rice) 49
West Africa: recipe 49

Z

Zeljanica (Filo pastry pie with spinach) 84
Zoute haring (Salted pickled herrings) 60

1 3 5 7 9 10 8 6 4 2

Published in 2019 by Ebury Press an imprint of Ebury Publishing,
20 Vauxhall Bridge Road,
London SW1V 2SA

Ebury Press is part of the Penguin Random House group of companies
whose addresses can be found at global.penguinrandomhouse.com

Text Copyright © Eurotunnel Le Shuttle 2019
Photography © Ian Garlick

Eurotunnel Le Shuttle has asserted its right to be identified as the author of this Work in
accordance with the Copyright, Designs and Patents Act 1988

info@eurotunnel.com
www.eurotunnel.com

This edition published by Ebury Press in 2019

www.penguin.co.uk

Project manager: Fiona Robbins
Food photographer: Ian Garlick
Recipe editorial: Wendy Sweetser, Hairy Bikers (page 24), Geoff Capes (page 15) and
Theo Randall (page 126)
Food stylist: Wendy Sweetser
Art direction and design: Emma King
Copy writers: Wendy Sweetser, Sam Bone and Jae Hopkins
Proofing and index: Aune Butt
Editorial assistant: Jae Hopkins
Additional photography: Eurotunnel Le Shuttle, Adobe Stock, Alamy Stock, Stephen Blake, Katie
Vermont, Emma King, Julia Becker, The Aspinall Foundation and Aurélie Four for @lecorgi

Recipes found in this publication have been tried,
tested and in some cases written by Wendy Sweetser,
professional food, wine and travel writer, on behalf of
Eurotunnel Le Shuttle

A CIP catalogue record for this book is available from the British Library

ISBN 9781529103304

Printed and bound in China by Toppan Leefung